Influencing TODAY'S YOUTH

Shaping the Behaviors, Expectations, and Aspirations of Tomorrow's Leaders

Dr. Danita Johnson Woods

Influencing Today's Youth
Shaping the Behaviors, Expectations, and Aspirations of Tomorrow's Leaders
by Dr. Danita Johnson Woods

ISBN: 979-8-9948280-0-7

Library of Congress Control Number: 2012937799

Published by: Vitality Ventures, Inc.
4506 Thornbury Dr. E., Valparaiso, IN 46383
United States of America

Second Edition

Printed in the United States of America

To purchase additional copies of this book, please visit
www.drdanitajohnsonwoods.com

Praise for *Influencing Today's Youth*

Debut author Woods writes of "transforming the world," via better communication with children.

Once an unwed teen mother herself, now a Ph.D. running a comprehensive integrated health care system, Woods writes frankly about how to discuss and model appropriate behavior on tough topics that routinely baffle both adults and children: obesity, education, sex and, above all, learning from mistakes.

Her approach is simple, direct, and honest. "If we don't talk about sex, our kids will find a way to talk about it anyway," she writes, urging the reader to take the path of greatest benefit instead of least resistance. But discussing those tough topics with young people does not mean treating them as adults. "They are going to be adults soon enough. Let them be kids while they can. In fact, insist upon it," Woods states. She reinforces the importance of connection and social responsibility with interviews of other community-centered professionals, occasionally punctuating her points with stories of extraordinary individuals who've chosen to step up and have an influence in a young person's life.

Woods has a knack for reducing complicated concepts to their basic principles, as when she explains that "influencing" kids boils down to being present, open, and acting responsibly. She's a strong voice speaking from within the community, not standing apart to reassure readers that they're able to really do good, right now. "Children, especially young children, learn through observation," Woods writes, reinforcing the importance of owning one's own actions. "Your words have value, but not as much value as your actions."

Woods' straightforward, honest approach makes potentially intimidating topics manageable.

—KIRKUS REVIEW

Author's Note

This book was originally written in 2012, during a time of rapid change in how children learned, communicated, and interacted with the world around them. Even then, it was clear that the pace of life was accelerating and that young people were growing up in an environment very different from the one many adults remembered.

Since that time, the forces shaping childhood and adolescence have intensified. Social media, smartphones, artificial intelligence, and a 24-hour digital ecosystem now influence how young people see themselves, relate to others, and make decisions, often long before adults recognize the impact. At the same time, families, educators, and caregivers are navigating unprecedented levels of stress, distraction, and uncertainty.

What has not changed is the fundamental truth at the heart of this book: children do not need more control; they need meaningful influence. They need adults who are present, grounded, values-driven, and willing to model the very behaviors they hope to see.

This updated edition builds upon *Influencing Today's Youth*, preserving its original voice and principles while offering substantive rewrites and added context to reflect today's realities. My goal is not to criticize young people or those raising them, but to equip adults with clarity, confidence, and practical insight in a world that often feels overwhelming.

Influence remains one of the most powerful, and underestimated tools we have. My hope is that this book continues to serve as a guide, an encouragement, and a reminder that positive influence, consistently applied, can shape lives in lasting ways.

— Dr. Danita Johnson Woods

To our youth—may you be influenced to find your way
and light the path for generations to come.

Contents

Introduction

"Things sure are different today compared to when I was a kid."

Have you ever heard yourself say these words? I've certainly said them, and I'm sure we all have at one point. That's because society and today's generation are different from when we were younger. However, different doesn't mean bad or good. It's just...well...different. And today, that difference feels wider and faster than ever before.

You don't have to look too hard to see the differences everywhere. From on-demand streaming and constant connectivity, to information at your fingertips via the Internet and mobile devices, today's youth are being raised in an extraordinarily fast-paced, high-tech world... one shaped by smartphones, social media, and algorithm-driven content... and the pace and speed of information will only increase as the years go by.

As a result, we see many traits in today's youth that are difficult for adults to understand, namely

- Many children appear increasingly comfortable relying on shortcuts, sometimes mistaking access to information for mastery of it. After all, why write a report on a topic when all the information is already there online about it, or when digital tools make it easy to bypass the learning process altogether? Today's youth are growing up in an environment that makes delayed gratification significantly harder to develop. Technology has created an "I want it now" culture.
- Neuroscience now confirms what many adults sense intuitively: constant digital stimulation conditions the brain to expect immediate feedback, making patience and perseverance harder skills to develop. In the past, children wrote letters (even had

pen pals), and they relied on landline telephones or face-to-face communication. From social media feeds to group chats and gaming platforms, today's youth are influenced in spaces that blend communication, entertainment, and identity. They get the answers they are seeking immediately and expect everything else to occur just as quickly.

- Too many children seem unwilling to risk failure. In today's world, failure often feels public and permanent; captured online, shared instantly, and judged quickly, making risk feel far more costly than it once did. Our "instant" culture has resulted in kids wanting not only quick and positive results, but they also want it for little effort. As such, many seem unwilling to stick with an endeavor for the long-term.

But here's the irony: As much as things have changed, they have also remained the same. The context is different, but the core questions remain timeless. The only difference is that the problems and challenges today occur at a different time and space. In other words, the external stimuli or factors that create the challenges are different (i.e. technological advances have created differences in the way kids learn, work, are socialized, etc.), but the questions surrounding kids and how we raise them are identical to the questions and challenges from generations ago, namely:

- How do we assure that our children receive a good education?
- How do we keep them safe?
- Who are their friends?
- How do we teach them to be civil in their interactions with others?

- How do we prepare them for future success?
- How do we influence them to be the best they can be?

The Art of Influence

The key to overcoming so many of today's challenges with youth can be summed up in one word: *Influence.*

When you properly influence young people, you can shape their behaviors, expectations, and aspirations. You're able to encourage positive social, emotional, and intellectual development, what we all want for today's children.

Influence is the quiet, ongoing power of presence, example, and intention that shapes how people see themselves, what they believe is possible, and how they choose to act, often long before outcomes are visible. Influence is not about control, popularity, or position. It is not measured by followers, titles, or applause. True influence is revealed in what remains after an interaction ends; the beliefs people carry forward, the standards they internalize, and the courage they borrow when they doubt themselves. Influence is an important word today. We influence others and are influenced by others daily. Influence comes from many sources: an advertisement on television promising you'll be slim in 60 days or less, a boss encouraging you to stretch your workplace skills, a schoolyard bully taunting another child, and even a sweet-faced toddler pouting to get another piece of candy.

Influence is everywhere. Today, it reaches children long before adults realize it and often with far more consistency. It's hard enough for you, as an adult, to manage the influences in the world. Think about what it's like for a young person who has not yet developed the tools needed to make a positive choice to manage the flood of influence bombarding him or her every day.

Obviously, not all influence is negative. And that's where you come in; to be a positive source of influence on the youth in your life, whether you're a parent, grandparent, aunt, uncle, teacher, coach, neighbor, or someone who works with or interacts with kids on a regular basis. Additionally, parents, caregivers, and other concerned adults can help by teaching kids to develop their own influence, also known as their internal GPS. Influence is the component of your GPS that instructs your values and reminds you of basic principles, like "Be kind to others." Influence is the bridge that leads to today's youth becoming tomorrow's productive citizens.

Influence is not about who you are to the world, it is about who someone becomes because you were in their life.

Influence versus Control

Realize that influencing a child does not mean exerting control over him or her. In fact, the more I work with parents and children, the more I realize that many of the challenges families face come down to a matter of control. The adult is attempting to control the youth rather than influence him. While control may work for young children, the older kids get, the less effective control is. Once the child becomes a teenager, it becomes a battle of wills, especially in a world where teens are already exercising autonomy online long before they are granted it at home.

While the parents' intent may be to provide security and safety for their children, Excessive control can unintentionally stifle the development of responsibility and independent decision-making. Of course, the solution isn't to turn over complete control to our children. There are obvious ramifications to this response. Children need the guidance and mentorship of an adult.

So, what is the balance between control and choice? *Influence.*

Reaching today's youth is not about telling them what to do, making them listen, or forcing them to respect you; it's about influencing them to want to be the best they can be. Realize that when you raise kids with strict control over their decisions and behavior, and then overnight expect them to be responsible adults when they come of legal age, you'll be disappointed. Influence isn't a one-time act. Rather, it's a long-term outlook and approach to interacting with youth. The good news is that no matter where you are on your parenting journey (or your relationship with the youth in your life), you can start influencing them today.

Why Influence?

As President and CEO of Edgewater Health, an integrated mental health and primary care organization serving Gary and Northwest Indiana, I have spent decades walking alongside individuals and families at some of their most vulnerable moments. I see firsthand the ripple effects that occur when support systems fray, when families are strained, communities are under pressure, and children grow up without consistent, positive guidance.

Most adults want the same thing for the children in their lives—to keep them safe, encourage them to be responsible, and help them succeed. In conversations with parents of teenagers, I often hear a familiar expression of concern: *"I just want my son—or daughter—to take responsibility for their actions."* It is a heartfelt wish, born of love and frustration. When we explore that concern together, it often opens a deeper reflection about the ways responsibility is learned, modeled, and reinforced over time.

Many parents realize in that moment that influence is not something that happens all at once or in a single conversation. It is built gradually through daily examples, expectations, and relationships. And when those influences are intentional, steady, and grounded in care, they can quietly shape choices long before challenges arise.

The fact is your words and actions, or the absence of them, shape how young people grow and respond to the world. Children cannot consistently demonstrate behaviors they have not had the opportunity to observe, practice, and internalize from the adults in their lives. So, if you want a child to be responsible, trusting, loving, mature, or kind (fill in the blank with the values that matter most to you), you must first model and influence those traits.

Many well-intentioned adults today are highly protective of children. Often described as *"helicopter parenting,"* this approach involves hovering closely over a child's experiences. More recently, experts have also identified *"snowplow parenting,"* where adults remove obstacles rather than prepare children to navigate them. While these approaches are rooted in care and concern, excessive protection can unintentionally limit the development of essential life skills such as responsibility, decision-making, emotional maturity, and resilience.

When adults intervene too quickly or too often, children are deprived of the opportunity to learn from choices, mistakes, and natural consequences. As a result, constant hovering, despite good intentions, does little to strengthen a child's ability to take ownership of their actions or make decisions grounded in strong values. The goal is not to step away, but to step alongside—modeling behavior, reinforcing values, and gradually transferring responsibility in age-appropriate ways.

Influence in Action: Protection vs. Preparation

One of the most powerful ways we influence children is through what we model, not what we demand. Like many parents and caregivers, I can recall moments when stress or emotion shaped the tone I used, times when I later wished I had responded differently. Those moments are part of being human. What matters most is not perfection, but awareness.

When children experience respect consistently, they learn what respect looks like in practice. Over time, they mirror what they see. If disrespect becomes frequent, even unintentionally, it is the behavior itself, not our intentions, that begins to shape their responses.

The same is true with listening. If we want children to listen with patience and care, they must first experience what it feels like to be heard. Influence is not immediate; it is cultivated through small, repeated interactions over time.

At its core, influence is simple. Children learn primarily through observation. Words matter, but actions matter more. What is modeled consistently becomes what is internalized.

Children also navigate competing influences from peers, media, and the world around them. When faced with choices, a child who has been allowed to observe responsibility, practice decision-making, and exercise age-appropriate independence, is better equipped to respond thoughtfully.

Mistakes will still happen. Children will test boundaries and misjudge situations. But those who have been shaped by steady, positive influences are far more capable of learning from those moments and continuing to grow.

Start from the Inside Out

We live in demanding times, filled with constant distractions for both adults and children. Amid the noise, what matters most is not perfection, but presence—how we show up, what we model, and what we make visible through our choices. At its core, meaningful influence looks like this:

1. **Be present.**
   We live in demanding times, filled with constant distractions for both adults and children. Being present does not mean

being perfect or always available, it means being intentional. Commit to showing up consistently, not only physically, but emotionally, by paying attention, listening, and responding with care.

2. **Be open.**
   Meaningful influence grows through communication. Openness requires curiosity, patience, and humility. Influence is not built through lecturing, shouting, or controlling outcomes, but through honest dialogue and mutual respect. Commit to creating space where your child feels safe to speak and where you are willing to listen.
3. **Be a role model.**
   Ultimately, influence is reinforced by example. What you do often carries more weight than what you say. When your actions align with your values, they send a powerful message, one that young people notice, remember, and often emulate.

I admit that I often worry for children with great potential who lack consistent guidance and steady support, the ones who have so much potential but don't have a beacon to guide their path, or an anchor to grasp when the challenges of life try to push them down. Fortunately, by reading this book and applying the information, you're making sure the children in your life are no longer "lost."

Yes, we live in challenging times. In a world overflowing with noise, competing voices, and constant stimulation, intentional influence has never mattered more. Children are not lacking information—they are lacking anchors.

Chapter One

A Defining Experience of Positive Influence

"Often, one person can influence a child to find something in herself and grow up to her full potential. When I was a child, one person showed me the power of positive influence and made that difference for me. You can be that person for someone else."
~ Dr. Danita Johnson Woods

When I was six years old, my family moved to a house on Polk Street in Gary, Indiana. Like many children experiencing change, I hoped the move might bring a fresh start. While our address changed, the challenges my family carried with us did not. Some families on Polk Street owned their homes and appeared more settled. We lived in the basement of someone else's house, doing the best we could with what we had.

Although childhood today looks different, smartphones replacing sidewalks and social media replacing neighborhood cliques, the core needs of children remain unchanged. Children still need to feel seen, valued, protected, and believed in. Positive influence mattered then, and it matters just as much now.

My parents shared one room, and my five siblings and I shared the other. Living in close quarters created moments of closeness among us, but it also reflected the strain my parents were under as they navigated limited resources, heavy responsibilities, and their own unresolved challenges. Children in the neighborhood noticed our differences, and sometimes those differences became the basis for teasing.

At the time, I didn't have words for concepts like trauma, stress, or emotional overload. I only knew what it felt like to live in an environment where tension was present and uncertainty was familiar. Like many children growing up in difficult circumstances, I carried more emotional weight than most people could see.

Looking back now, I recognize that my parents were shaped by their own histories, expectations, and the norms of their time. With time and perspective, I have come to understand that my parents were doing the best they could with what they knew, and that love and struggle often coexist in complicated ways. That understanding does not erase the impact of those years, but it allows me to hold the story with compassion.

Bullying compounded the weight I was already carrying. Teasing followed us to school and sometimes escalated into intimidation or physical harm. I remember being afraid to go to school, wishing I could disappear for a while just to avoid the stares and whispers. Today, we understand how chronic stress and instability affect a child's ability to feel safe, focus, and learn. At six years old, I only knew that I was scared.

What I needed during that time was not rescue, but stability, someone who could offer consistency when much of life felt unpredictable. One such person was Mrs. Kaufman.

Mrs. Kaufman was my first-grade teacher at Douglas Elementary. In my memory, she stands out not only for her warmth and intelligence, but for the way she consistently made me feel important. She noticed my work. She encouraged my creativity. And when I struggled, she offered reassurance instead of dismissal.

"That's a beautiful picture, Danita. You're so creative with colors."

"Good penmanship, Danita. Keep it up."

And when I came in alone from the playground, looking discouraged:

"Don't you worry, Danita. A nice girl like you will make lots of friends. Sometimes it just takes a while. You wait and see."

One day she asked if I would like to stay after school and help her. In today's language, Mrs. Kaufman would be called a protective adult, someone who shows up consistently and intentionally in a child's life. At the time, I didn't have words for it. I only knew that being near her made me feel safe and capable.

What Mrs. Kaufman offered me—without ever naming it—was a safe, consistent adult presence. She did not change my circumstances, but she buffered me from their weight. Her consistency gave me something I desperately needed: stability and belief.

At the time, I didn't understand the significance of what she was giving me—but years later, I've come to see how influence often works.

Influence Is Often Invisible

Most influence leaves no paper trail.
There is no certificate for the moment a teenager decides not to quit.
No applause when a child remembers how you treated someone else and chooses kindness instead.
Influence often works quietly—long before outcomes are visible.
A listening ear becomes courage years later.
A consistent presence becomes stability in chaos.
A single sentence, spoken in the right moment, can echo for a lifetime.
You may never know the full impact of your influence.
But that does not diminish its power.

A lot of children would have disliked staying after class. But I didn't mind. It was preferable to being teased on the walk home or returning to a crowded house where quiet space was hard to find. Staying after school wasn't about extra work, it was about being in the presence of an adult who made me feel seen and safe.

Mrs. Kaufman treated me with dignity. She trusted me with responsibility. She even paid me a dime for helping her—my first experience earning money for my effort. I remember the shine and weight of those coins, and the pride they brought. They represented independence and possibility.

When she noticed my worn shoes, she quietly offered me a new pair—without embarrassment or pity. They were beautiful red canvas slip-ons, simple and sturdy, yet more special than anything I had owned. Their bright color felt bold to me, almost daring, as if they announced a confidence I hadn't yet learned how to claim.

Mrs. Kaufman framed the gift in a way that preserved my dignity, making it clear that I was contributing value, not receiving charity. She explained that they were extra—unneeded by someone else—and that I should have them. That distinction mattered. She gave without making me feel small.

Mrs. Kaufman gave me much more than shoes or spare change. She modeled consistency, fairness, and belief. She showed me that adults could be safe, encouraging, and invested. Years later, I would understand that moments like that—quiet, practical, and filled with respect—were teaching me how confidence is built, one small step at a time.

Why do I tell you this story?

Because Mrs. Kaufman represents what intentional influence can look like, especially when it arrives at a moment of need. She was not the only influence in my life, nor was influence absent before or after her. But her presence helped shape how I understood myself and what I believed was possible.

Because of that belief, I didn't give up on myself. My challenges did not disappear, and my circumstances did not change overnight. But I stayed engaged. I returned to school. I continued learning and growing.

In an era of data dashboards, test scores, algorithms, and risk assessments, it is easy to lose sight of the individual child standing in front of us. But you don't influence numbers, you influence people. Influence begins with intention, presence, and belief.

Whether the young person in your life is a child, niece, nephew, grandchild, student, or neighbor, you can be a steady influence. Sometimes that influence shows up in big gestures. More often, it appears in small, consistent ones.

This is how we begin to influence not just one child—but many. Quietly. Intentionally. One life at a time.

The Quiet Power of Being That Person

Pause and think about the adults who shaped your early years—not those with titles, but those who offered steadiness when life felt uncertain.

Who noticed you when you felt overlooked?
Who spoke to you with respect before you believed you deserved it?
Who offered consistency when circumstances were unpredictable?

Now turn inward.

In the lives of young people around you, how do you show up? What do they experience in your presence—pressure or patience, judgment or belief?

Positive influence does not require perfection or grand gestures. It begins with attention, consistency, and the decision to be safe and intentional.

You may never see the outcome of your influence.
You may never know which moment mattered most.
But presence, offered repeatedly and without condition,
takes root.

Sit with this truth:
Being "that person" is not about changing a child's circumstances.
It is about changing how they see themselves within their circumstances.

Closing Reflection

Positive influence rarely announces itself. It grows through consistency, patience, and care. It is shaped by everyday moments—by how we speak, how we listen, and how we show up when it matters most.

When adults choose to be present and intentional, they help children carry forward something that lasts far beyond childhood: belief.

Reflection Question

Who has been a defining influence in your life—and how might you become that presence for a young person today?

In the chapters that follow, we will explore how influence shows up in families, schools, health, education, and community life—because the need for intentional influence has never been greater than it is today.

Chapter Two

It's Everyone's Responsibility to Influence the Future

"You can never really live anyone else's life, not even your child's. The influence you exert is through your own life, and what you've become yourself."
~ Eleanor Roosevelt

Responsibility as the Foundation of Influence

The more you influence today's children, the more you contribute to shaping the future of our world. Influence does not begin with grand gestures or sweeping reforms; it begins much closer to home. Real change starts when we take responsibility for the circumstances within our immediate sphere of influence.

We begin to affect our circumstances more powerfully when we connect meaningfully with others. Those connections deepen when we understand ourselves—our values, our blind spots, and our responsibilities. None of this is possible without a willingness to take ownership. Taking responsibility for influencing today's youth begins with taking responsibility for ourselves and for the role we play in the world around us. Whatever change you hope to see in your community, your family, your nation, or yourself, there comes a moment when progress requires you to say, *"This begins with me."*

Today, responsibility is often diffused, shifted to systems, institutions, algorithms, policies, or an unnamed "someone else." Many people feel overwhelmed by the complexity of the challenges facing our children and are uncertain about where their influence even begins. That uncertainty is understandable. It is also precisely why personal responsibility matters now more than ever.

All of us influence others every day, whether we intend to or not. But the influence that shapes lives most powerfully is not accidental. It is intentional. Choosing to be a positive influence requires conscious effort and accountability. In a world filled with constant noise, competing narratives, and endless distraction, influence requires intentionality: choosing presence over passivity, reflection over reaction, and action over commentary.

Responsibility operates on three interconnected levels: **personal, proximal, and social.** Together, they form the framework through which lasting influence is built.

The Three Levels of Responsibility

1) Personal Responsibility

Personal responsibility begins with introspection. To take responsibility for your actions and outcomes, you must first understand who you are and what you value. When you accept personal responsibility, you set goals that help you grow while also benefiting others. You seek out the information, skills, and relationships necessary to pursue those goals. And you take action without waiting for permission or relying on others to move first.

In today's environment, personal responsibility also includes how we manage information, regulate emotions, and model balance in a fast-paced, digitally driven world. Children are watching how adults respond to stress, disagreement, failure, and success. What we model becomes part of what they internalize.

Taking responsibility does not mean labeling yourself as good or bad based on outcomes. It means being accountable for doing your best, learning from success, addressing failure honestly, and making necessary adjustments along the way. When things go well, you accept the rewards. When they don't, you accept the consequences and commit to improvement. Responsibility is neither self-blame nor external blame; it is ownership with purpose.

People who take personal responsibility tend to remain open to new ideas, to other people, and to growth. They understand that results require effort and that setbacks are part of progress. They meet both opportunity and difficulty with perspective and grace.

2) Proximal Responsibility

Proximal responsibility refers to the responsibility we have toward those closest to us, family members, friends, neighbors, coworkers, and peers. It involves offering encouragement when actions are constructive, sharing information that supports growth, and providing honest feedback when behavior has negative consequences.

When reaching out feels uncomfortable, intrusive, or inconvenient, it can be tempting to withdraw under the belief that we are not responsible for one another. And it's true. We are not accountable for every choice others make. But people do not thrive in isolation. Influence depends on connection.

In an age where many relationships are mediated by digital screens and online platforms, proximal responsibility reminds us that meaningful influence still happens through real presence like showing up, listening carefully, speaking truthfully, and staying engaged even when it would be easier to step back. When we fail to support others despite having the ability to do so, we weaken not only their growth, but our own support systems as well. Each act of engagement strengthens the relational fabric of our closest circles, shaping the communities we become.

3) Social Responsibility

Social responsibility reflects our shared obligation to contribute to the well-being of the larger community. Those who embrace this level of responsibility understand that change at the societal level ultimately affects individuals, children, families, and neighborhoods. By working toward the common good, they strengthen the conditions that allow everyone a better chance to thrive.

Social responsibility requires moving beyond complaint and blame to ask a more productive question: *What can I do to influence this issue in a constructive way?* In today's climate, it also means resisting the urge to substitute visibility for impact—to confuse awareness with action.

People who take social responsibility recognize that everything we contribute, or fail to contribute, adds to the environment our children grow up in. When we act with care, fairness, and intention, we make it easier for others to do the same. When we disengage, demean, or spread harm, even casually, we increase the burden for everyone.

An Integrated Approach

It can be tempting to view the three levels of responsibility, personal, proximal, and social, as separate or even optional. It's easy to believe that excelling in one area somehow compensates for neglecting the others. Personal responsibility, after all, often feels like the logical starting point, and it is foundational. Every meaningful journey begins with an individual decision to act.

But if the goal is to truly influence today's youth, these three levels cannot operate in isolation. Each one reinforces the others. In healthy individuals, families, organizations, and communities, personal responsibility strengthens proximal responsibility, proximal responsibility supports social responsibility, and social responsibility, in turn, creates conditions that make personal responsibility more attainable for everyone.

If every person consistently took responsibility for their own actions, there would be far less need for others to step in. If everyone tended carefully to their own corner of the world, many larger problems would resolve themselves. But experience tells us that waiting for universal accountability is neither realistic nor effective. The question, then, is not *whether* responsibility should be shared, but *how* it must be integrated.

The truth is that the actions of those with greater stability, access, or influence often make it easier—or harder—for others to take responsibility for themselves. When stronger individuals, families, or institutions act responsibly, they lower barriers for those who are struggling. When they do not, they increase those barriers.

You may not see yourself as one of the "stronger" people. You may feel stretched, tired, or unsure whether you have anything extra to give. But if you are reading this book, chances are you already have influence—through your position, your experience, your voice, or your presence. And influence carries responsibility.

As the Scripture reminds us: *"For everyone to whom much is given, from him much will be required."* (Luke 12:48) This is not a burden meant to induce guilt; it is a reminder that ability and responsibility are often linked.

Our individual choices rarely stay contained within our own lives. What we do in our corner of the world inevitably affects someone else's. When we consume more, someone else bears the environmental cost. When we disengage from civic life, someone else absorbs the consequences. When we model care, accountability, and restraint, we make those behaviors more accessible to the next generation.

In this way, personal responsibility becomes social responsibility, and social responsibility circles back to the individual. Proximal responsibility, the relationships closest to us, acts as the bridge between the two. It is through one-to-one connection that values are transmitted, accountability is reinforced, and influence becomes real.

Responsibility Is Not the Same as Blame

Responsibility does not mean carrying guilt for what you did not choose.
It means choosing how you respond to what you've been given.

You may not be responsible for your starting point—
your childhood, your trauma, your disadvantages, or your losses.
But you are responsible for the direction you move from here.

Taking responsibility is not harsh.
It is freeing.

Because the moment you claim responsibility, you reclaim your power to choose and influence follows.

At some point, each of us must face the consequences of our choices alone. No one can do that work for us. At the same time, others will inevitably experience the ripple effects of our decisions. We live in relationship with one another, and influence, whether intentional or not, is unavoidable.

Many of the challenges we see today in families, schools, organizations, and communities can be traced back to a breakdown at one or more of these levels of responsibility. Progress does not require perfection, but it does require integration. When personal ownership, relational accountability, and collective responsibility work together, influence becomes sustainable and change becomes possible.

The Roots of Responsibility

I was not responsible for being born economically disadvantaged, nor was I responsible for growing up in a household shaped by instability, neglect, and harmful patterns. Today, we better understand how early trauma and chronic stress can influence behavior, opportunity, and decision-making. Still, there came a point when I had to decide what I would do with the circumstances I had been given. As an adult, I had to choose what kind of life I would build.

At first, I spent time blaming others for my problems and setbacks. As a young single mother cleaning bedpans at a psychiatric hospital, I carried a great deal of anger. Some of that anger was understandable. But regardless of its origin, it was not helping me move forward. It only drained energy that could have been used to build a better future. Today, that same kind of unresolved anger often shows up in different forms, e.g., comparison, blame, or constant outrage, but the effect is the same.

If I was going to create a different life, I had to take responsibility for it. I didn't know yet what direction to go, but I knew I couldn't do it alone. That meant learning how to ask for help, accept guidance, and contribute something in return. The first real shift was internal: I had to change how I saw myself and my possibilities.

That wasn't easy. Growing up, I had limited examples of healthy personal, proximal, or social responsibility. My parents were navigating their own limitations within the norms and constraints of their time, doing the best they could with what they understood and what was available to them. Like many adults of their generation, they carried unresolved burdens that shaped how responsibility was expressed, or, at times, avoided, in our home.

My mother's life unfolded within expectations that left her economically and socially dependent, with few viable paths toward independence.

She left my father more than once, an instinct that reflected courage and a desire for change, even when the resources and support needed to sustain that change were scarce. With distance and perspective, I have come to understand her as a woman constrained by fear, circumstance, and the realities of her era. That understanding does not erase the impact of those years, but it allows me to hold her story with compassion.

My father struggled in different ways. He often felt overtaken by forces beyond his control and was not consistently present in the ways a family needs. His absence, volatility, and misuse of authority shaped my early understanding of responsibility—not through guidance, but through contrast. Some of my earliest lessons came from observing what did not work, and from quietly resolving to choose differently when I had the chance.

With time, I have come to see that responsibility is often learned not only through what we are given, but through what we are determined to become.

Without consistent examples, my siblings and I entered adulthood with more questions than guidance when it came to navigating relationships. Some of us revisited familiar patterns before learning how to release them. I eventually understood that while I could acknowledge the impact of my upbringing, I could not allow it to dictate my future. At a certain point, responsibility becomes a choice—one made deliberately, again and again.

Here is where social responsibility also matters. The limited opportunities available to women during my mother's lifetime, the lack of legal protections, and the normalization of abuse all contributed to the environment in which she felt trapped. Systems failed her—and us. Understanding that does not remove personal accountability, but it does remind us that responsibility exists at multiple levels.

My own progress is proof that personal responsibility, supported by the right influences, can interrupt even deeply rooted patterns. Along the way, I sought out people who modeled honesty, consistency, and care.

One of those people was my grandmother. She was not demonstrative, but she was clear. She named harmful behavior for what it was and affirmed my worth. Her guidance, simple and direct, became a stabilizing influence in my life. Over time, others offered counsel that reinforced those early lessons. Small seeds, planted by the right people, made a lasting difference.

Personal responsibility is easier to sustain when it is supported by proximal responsibility, by people who tell the truth, offer encouragement, and remain invested in your growth. This requires discernment. Not every voice deserves access to your inner circle. Choose relationships that challenge you constructively, not destructively.

Belief in yourself does not arrive fully formed. It is built gradually, through effort and persistence. Sometimes it begins with nothing more than the desire for something better. Once movement begins, clarity follows. Growth is rarely linear, but it is possible.

Influence works the same way. It begins with a single, intentional step.

Pay It Forward

Throughout my life, others influenced me in ways that shaped my ability to grow, lead, and serve. Today, in my professional work, I see daily evidence that people, especially young people. need positive influences to survive, stabilize, and eventually thrive.

That understanding is what drew me to leadership in a struggling community mental health center years ago. By strengthening accountability, systems, and relationships, we created change that extended beyond individuals to families and communities. That kind of influence is deeply rewarding.

I would not be where I am today without those who stepped in when I needed guidance. Now, with experience and resources, I take on broader social responsibility because I am able to do so. Influence carries obligation, not as guilt, but as purpose.

Helping others does not always happen through formal programs. Sometimes it happens simply by exposing a young person to a possibility they had never imagined.

Helping others strengthens the world in ways we cannot always measure. Influence does not always come through systems, structures, or planned interventions. Often, it happens quietly, through access, encouragement, and example.

When adults choose to take responsibility at the personal, proximal, and social levels, they create pathways for young people to imagine possibilities they may not yet see for themselves. This is how influence multiplies—one decision, one relationship, one moment at a time.

Responsibility is not theoretical—it is lived. Once we understand how personal, proximal, and social responsibility intersect, the question is no longer *whether* we influence young people, but *how.* Influence becomes most powerful when responsibility moves from concept to practice, from intention to action. In the chapters that follow, we will look more closely at where that responsibility shows up in everyday life and how small, consistent choices can shape outcomes far beyond what we can immediately see.

Influence the Future

Now that you understand how personal, proximal, and social responsibility work together, the question becomes practical: *Where can your influence matter most*? The chapters that follow will explore that question.

Remember, influence does not require perfection or position. Even small, consistent actions can shape a young person at a critical moment. Believe that your presence matters, because it does.

Responsibility Begins Here

Pause and consider the people who influenced you, not only through what they said, but through how they lived.

What did you learn about responsibility by watching the adults around you?
What behaviors were modeled clearly—and what lessons were left unspoken?
Where did you learn to take ownership, and where did you learn to withdraw, deflect, or endure?

Responsibility is rarely taught in isolation. It is absorbed through example, reinforced through relationships, and shaped by circumstance. Over time, it becomes either a burden we avoid or a strength we claim.

Sit with this truth:
You may not be responsible for everything that shaped you,
but you are responsible for what you choose to shape next.
Influence begins not with control, but with ownership; quiet, consistent, and intentional.

Closing Reflection

Responsibility is the quiet bridge between influence and impact. It begins internally, extends outward, and eventually reshapes communities. When we take responsibility for our own choices, we strengthen our capacity to support others. When we support those closest to us, we build trust. And when trust grows, collective responsibility becomes possible.

Influencing the future does not require perfection, power, or position. It requires willingness, the willingness to stop waiting, to stop deflecting, and to step forward with intention. Every generation is shaped by those who decide that what happens next matters enough to act.

If we want better outcomes for our children, we must first model what responsibility looks like in real life: ownership, consistency, courage, and care. The future is not influenced by words alone, but by the choices we are willing to stand behind.

Reflection Question

Which level of responsibility, personal, proximal, or social, are you being called to strengthen right now, and what is one intentional step you can take this week to act on it?

Chapter Three

Influence Youth to Embrace a Sense of Family

"Feelings of worth can flourish only in an atmosphere where individual differences are appreciated, mistakes are tolerated, communication is open, and rules are flexible—the kind of atmosphere that is found in a nurturing family."
~ Virginia Satir

In an increasingly complex and fast-moving world, a sense of family remains one of the most powerful stabilizing forces in a young person's life. Family, at its best, offers children belonging, guidance, accountability, and a place where they are known beyond their performance or potential. It is often the first environment where values are learned, identity is shaped, and resilience begins to take root.

When families function as they should, children are better equipped to navigate life's challenges. They learn how to manage emotions, build relationships, and imagine a future for themselves. But when families are unable, because of stress, instability, absence, or unmet needs, to provide consistent support and healthy influence, children do not stop seeking connection. They simply look elsewhere.

Every young person searches for a sense of family. That search is instinctive. When the foundation is missing at home, children will often create or attach themselves to alternative systems of belonging, some constructive, others harmful. The question is not whether children will connect, but where and to whom.

This is where influence becomes critical.

Concerned adults, parents, extended family members, teachers, mentors, neighbors, coaches, and community leaders, can step into the gap. A sense of family does not require biological ties. It is built through presence, trust, shared values, and consistency over time. Any adult willing to show up with care and intention can influence a young person to experience belonging, accountability, and stability.

Family, in this broader sense, is about connection and commitment. It is about teaching values such as honesty, respect, loyalty, responsibility, and care for others. When children experience these qualities, wherever they are modeled, they begin to see themselves as worthy, capable, and connected. That belief becomes a foundation upon which healthy decisions and hopeful futures are built.

When adults choose to invest in relationships with youth and engage with the communities they live in, they do more than offer support. They help redefine what family can mean. And when children begin to believe they matter, they become open to imagining options, making choices, and pursuing paths that lead toward stability and success.

Influence in Action

At this point, people often wonder whether an adult who has no biological connection to a child can truly help that child embrace a sense of family. The answer is yes, because family is built through presence, consistency, and trust, not DNA alone.

One of the clearest examples I have seen is Brandon Freeland, a single young man who has never been married and who has taken on the responsibility of being a steady, father-like influence to two boys, John and Kevin, each for very different reasons. I know Brandon through my work at Edgewater Health, and what stands out about him is not perfection, but commitment. He understood something research and real life both confirm: children do not need flawless adults; they need reliable ones.

Here are their stories.

John

When John was fourteen, he began living with Brandon. By that age, John already had a history of arrests and juvenile delinquency and was well known to the local court system and law enforcement. He lived with his mother and extended family in unstable housing situations, public housing and short-term rentals that rarely felt secure. Family dynamics were strained, and John was often labeled a troublemaker and a thief. Over time, he internalized the message that he was on his own. By fourteen, he was committing robberies and selling drugs.

Brandon had gotten to know John's family through work he was doing in the community. He saw firsthand how instability, conflict, and lack of consistent guidance were pushing John toward the streets. He began speaking with John regularly about choices, consequences, and what it means to become a productive citizen.

One summer, John's family needed to move but had nowhere stable to go in between homes. Because Brandon had become close to the family, he offered for John to stay with him for a few days. Those days became weeks when John's mother was arrested on an active warrant. Brandon did not want John back on the streets, and other family members were scattered with friends. So Brandon let John stay longer and made sure John went to school and stayed out of trouble.

When John's mother was released, John returned home. Almost immediately, he began missing school and getting into trouble again. John told Brandon he wanted to do better, but he felt like he had to make his own way, and fast.

That is when Brandon made a decision that changed everything. He offered John a place to stay again, with clear expectations: go to school, stay out of trouble, and follow the rules of the home. John agreed and worked hard to keep his word.

Brandon did not allow all-night wandering, drugs, or skipped school. When John tested limits, as teenagers do, Brandon stayed consistent. He corrected, coached, encouraged, and modeled the kind of stability John had rarely experienced.

John had not seen his biological father since he was six and had few memories of him. Brandon became an example of what a responsible, productive man looks like, without criminality, absence, or chaos.

John stayed with Brandon for the next five years. He had typical teenage pushback, but he kept his promise to stay in school and stay out of trouble. Today, John is in college working toward his associate's degree. The influence Brandon provided, and the sense of family he created, gave John direction. Without it, John's future could have followed a far more limited and painful path.

Kevin

Kevin's mother was one of Brandon's close friends from high school. When Kevin was born, she and her fiancé asked Brandon to be Kevin's godfather. Brandon accepted gladly, looking forward to being present in Kevin's life.

They were planning a wedding. But two weeks before the ceremony, Kevin's father was arrested on serious charges. That moment became a turning point, not only for the family, but for the kind of role Brandon would play.

Kevin's mother took the situation hard. She became depressed, withdrawn, and isolated. Most days she stayed inside, and Kevin became an unusually fretful baby. Brandon began picking Kevin up on weekends for church, outings, and steady routines. Then weekends became weekdays. Soon Brandon was picking Kevin up from daycare and keeping him until his mother got off work.

Over time, Brandon became far more than a ceremonial godparent. He potty trained Kevin, watched his first steps, checked homework, attended school programs, and provided structure when needed. Early on, Kevin even began calling him "Daddy," not because Brandon demanded it, but because children name what feels safe.

By the time Kevin was nine, his biological father had been released and re-jailed multiple times. Aside from Brandon, a grandfather, and an uncle, Kevin had few positive male role models.

Eventually, Kevin's mother regained stability, became a registered nurse, and rebuilt her emotional footing. That mattered. But Brandon believed his consistent presence during Kevin's most vulnerable years also mattered deeply. He understood Kevin was at risk of becoming "a statistic," and he was determined to interrupt that trajectory.

Today, Kevin is a "B" student and is described as polite, respectful, and appreciative. He still has growing to do, but he is on the right track. Without Brandon's influence, Kevin's story might have been very different.

When Love Is Limited

Some people love you, but cannot lead you.
Some are present, but not safe.
Some provide food, but not tenderness.
Structure, but not peace.

Recognizing limitation does not erase harm,
but it can free you from repeating it.
You can tell the truth and choose healing.
And you can build what you did not receive.

What These Stories Teach

What matters most in both of these stories is that Brandon functioned the way healthy family is supposed to function. He stayed.

He was not an "in and out" presence or a quick fix. He committed for the long haul, through setbacks, resistance, and the slow work of building trust. That consistency is crucial, because when adults show up briefly and disappear, it can reinforce a child's belief that no one is dependable.

Grandmother Moment

Even so, like John and Kevin, I found other supporters, people who helped me learn what family could mean. I can still see my grandmother, my father's mother, going nose to nose with her son on my behalf. He was decades younger and much taller, but she did not flinch.

After my father had told me, again, "You'll never amount to anything," my grandmother appeared. She walked right up to him, pressed a finger into his chest, and said, "You leave that child alone. She's okay." Then she turned to me and said, "Don't you listen to him. You can do anything."

In that moment, that tiny older woman was larger than life.

She was my champion, ten feet tall in my eyes.

Her courage did something simple and permanent. It told me my father's voice did not have to become my inner voice.

My grandmother loved her son, but she did not protect his behavior. She was honest. She spoke truth in real time. My father may not have benefited from it, but I did. It helped me form the beginnings of self-esteem and a sense of family strong enough to build on. Over time, I learned to create my own circle of support outside my family of origin.

Even today, I am intentional about who I trust and who I allow close. Trusting myself to choose well has sometimes been an uphill climb. But I come back, again and again, to the image of my grandmother telling me I was not what someone else said I was.

And I thank God for the people who saw more in me than my circumstances suggested, people who looked at a child and saw potential, not a prediction.

What my grandmother gave me in that moment was more than protection. She gave me a definition of family rooted in presence, courage, and truth. She showed me that family can be formed when someone is willing to stand between harm and a child, and to speak life where doubt has taken hold. Not every child has a grandmother who will do that, but every child needs someone who will. That is why a sense of family cannot be left to biology alone. It must be built intentionally.

A Family Affair

If you're a parent, it's your job to help your children experience a sense of family, belonging, boundaries, love, and accountability. If you're not a parent, you can still help instill that sense of family in the young people around you. You can become part of a child's support system as they work to overcome instability and find their way forward.

This matters now more than ever, because today's children face a bigger obstacle course than a generation ago. They are exposed earlier—to adult language, adult imagery, adult expectations, and adult problems. They move through a world of constant connectivity and constant comparison. Friendship, identity, and belonging are shaped not only at school and in neighborhoods, but through group chats, feeds, and digital spaces where influence is relentless.

At the same time, children are expected to learn more, adapt faster, and manage more pressure than ever. The learning curve is steeper, and distractions are more sophisticated. It is not an easy time to be a parent, a concerned adult, or a child.

In the face of these pressures, some parents disengage, not always out of selfishness, but often out of exhaustion, discouragement, or lack of support. When parents are absent, discipline and guidance suffer. When parents are present but overwhelmed or emotionally unprepared, children can experience neglect, inconsistency, or harm.

Yet the fundamentals remain: parenting has never been easy, and there has never been a simple rulebook for raising children in an ever-changing world.

I see these issues every day in my work in healthcare. Sometimes parents are present but stretched thin. Sometimes they are absent. Many grandmothers are raising their children's children. Children are doing their best to grow up in systems that often feel unstable.

So what's the solution?

First: adults must commit to involvement. There is no shortcut. If you're a parent, you must put in the time. If you're not, you can still invest through mentorship, community programs, and consistent presence.

Second: stay engaged with school. Know how your children are doing. Build relationships with teachers. That partnership becomes part of a child's safety net.

Third: know their circle—who they spend time with, and who has access to their attention and identity, both in person and online. Children need structure, boundaries, and guidance. Being a child's friend is not the same as being their anchor.

Children fear chaos, and there is plenty of it in their world. That is why listening matters. Children need a sounding board, but they also need adults who respond with wisdom—not as peers, but as role models.

Kids are dealing with rejection, pressure, bullying, violence, grief, and loss—sometimes earlier than we realize. They need a sense of family so they can cope. They need adults who can teach resilience, self-control, communication, and the ability to set goals and keep going.

A strong sense of family is often the first environment where these life skills take root. Schools cannot do this alone. Children learn these skills through role modeling and real-life support.

We must set limits for our kids, because they won't do it for themselves. We must provide real consequences when rules are broken. And we must resist rushing children into adulthood. Let them be kids as long as they can—because time to grow is part of what makes adulthood healthier later.

Encourage effort. Don't celebrate mediocrity. Help them compete with themselves, not just others. And most of all, let children be themselves. Don't burden them with unfulfilled adult expectations. Give them safety, space, and support to become their own best selves.

It's not easy. But it is the job we accept when we choose to influence a child.

Who Spoke for You?

Pause for a moment and think about the voices that shaped you early.

Who spoke up for you when you could not speak for yourself?

Who countered what was said over you and reminded you of what was true?
Who made you feel safe enough to keep becoming?

Now turn the question outward.

For the young people around you, whose voice are you becoming?
Do your words steady them or weigh them down
When a child is misunderstood or mislabeled, are you willing to speak with clarity and care?

Sit with this truth.
A child does not need everyone to understand them.
They need at least one adult who will stand close, speak wisely, and stay.

Closing Reflection

Choosing Family, Choosing Influence

Family is not defined solely by biology, proximity, or obligation. It is defined by presence, consistency, and care over time. For some children, family is found at home. For others, it is discovered through mentors, teachers, neighbors, grandparents, coaches, or community members who choose to show up when it matters most.

A strong sense of family gives children more than comfort; it gives them grounding. It teaches them who they are, that they matter, and how they belong in the world. When children know they are valued, they are better equipped to face challenges, recover from setbacks, and imagine a future larger than their circumstances.

Influencing a child to embrace a sense of family does not require perfection. It requires commitment. It requires adults willing to be present, to model values, to set boundaries with care, and to stay when things become difficult. Sometimes influence comes quietly through consistency. Sometimes it arrives boldly through advocacy. Either way, it leaves a lasting imprint.

As adults, we have the power to interrupt harmful patterns and create new ones. When we choose to influence with intention, honesty, and compassion, we offer children something enduring, a foundation they can build upon long after our direct involvement has ended.

Reflection Question

Who was (or could be) part of your chosen family—and how has their influence shaped who you are, or who you are becoming?

A sense of family gives children a place to stand—but it does not, by itself, teach them how to care for their bodies, manage stress, or sustain well-being over time. Belonging creates safety, yet growth requires guidance in daily choices that shape health and resilience. Once children feel supported, influence continues through the habits they observe, practice, and carry forward. This is where intention meets action.

Chapter Four

Influence Youth to Adopt Healthy Habits

"It is health that is real wealth and not pieces of gold and silver."
~ Mohandas Gandhi

No one wants to see children, many of whom are already struggling with health concerns related to weight, grow into adults facing preventable conditions that persist over time and limit both quality of life and potential. Yet despite growing awareness, the problem continues to escalate.

According to the Centers for Disease Control and Prevention, childhood obesity remains a serious public health concern in the United States. Approximately one in five children and adolescents between the ages of two and nineteen meet the criteria for obesity, with prevalence increasing steadily over the past two decades. These trends are not confined to individual families. They reflect broader patterns shaped by environment, access, education, and opportunity.

Obesity rates also vary across racial and ethnic groups, with higher prevalence among Hispanic children and children who identify as Black and are not Hispanic, compared with White and Asian children who are not Hispanic. These disparities are not driven by race itself, but by longstanding inequities in access to healthy food, safe spaces for physical activity, quality healthcare, and health education.

Why this matters to parents and adults is clear. When children experience obesity, they are more likely than their peers to face health conditions both in childhood and later in life, including elevated blood pressure and high cholesterol, increased risk of impaired glucose tolerance and Type 2 diabetes, breathing problems such as sleep apnea and asthma, joint discomfort, musculoskeletal strain, and metabolic conditions such as fatty liver disease. Children who experience obesity are also more likely to become adults who struggle with obesity and related health challenges.

Beyond physical health, obesity in childhood and adolescence is associated with social and emotional consequences. Discrimination, stigma, and low self-esteem can follow children into adulthood, affecting confidence, relationships, and opportunity.

Adult obesity is associated with serious health conditions, including heart disease, diabetes, and some cancers. When obesity begins in childhood, it is often more severe in adulthood. These patterns do not reflect individual failure. They reflect broader inequities in access to resources that support health over time.

Even when families technically have choices about what food enters the home, many caregivers face real barriers to making healthier ones consistently. Some lack access to nutrition education, time, or resources. Others are balancing demanding work schedules, multiple jobs, or caregiving responsibilities of their own. In those circumstances, quick and affordable options such as donuts, packaged meals, or highly processed foods can feel like the only practical choice, even when parents understand those options may not be ideal.

Many parents want to do better but have not been taught how nutrition affects concentration, immunity, or health over time. Reading food labels, planning balanced meals, and preparing vegetables in ways children will actually eat are learned skills, not intuitive ones. Even when families can afford healthier foods, they may not have the time, energy, or knowledge to prepare them in ways that fit daily life. Over time, these patterns can become deeply ingrained, not because of indifference, but because of exhaustion and limited support.

In my work leading Edgewater Health, an integrated healthcare system providing behavioral health and primary care services, I see the consequences of these challenges every day. Adults and children alike live with physical and mental health conditions associated with poor nutrition and limited physical activity. I see obesity and diabetes alongside depression and anxiety, as well as increased vulnerability to infection and chronic illness. These challenges affect individuals and families, but they also affect workplaces and communities. As a healthcare leader and employer, I see higher absenteeism, reduced productivity, and increased strain on systems meant to support well-being.

Many individuals initially seek care for mental health concerns, yet physical health needs often emerge alongside them. This is not surprising, because mental and physical health are deeply interconnected. Individuals living with serious mental illness are at higher risk for conditions such as hypertension, diabetes, heart disease, and cardiopulmonary problems. Some medications used to manage serious mental illness can also contribute to other medical complications, including weight gain, metabolic conditions, and side effects related to movement.

These realities reinforce an essential truth. Supporting healthy individuals requires a whole person approach to care. Mental and physical health cannot be treated in isolation. Lasting outcomes depend on coordinated, timely, and responsive services that address the full context of a person's life.

Health Is Learned at Home First

Long before health appears in charts, diagnoses, or policy debates, it is shaped in everyday moments, what is served at the table, how stress is handled, whether movement is part of daily life, and how rest is valued.

Children do not learn health from warnings or guidelines alone. They learn it by watching the adults around them. When home environments, even imperfect ones, model care, balance, and intention, children begin to experience health as part of life, not merely a response to crisis.

A National Health Crisis

Today, the nation faces an epidemic of childhood obesity. At a time when medical care continues to grow more expensive, we cannot afford to ignore preventable health risks that place unnecessary strain on individuals, families, and communities. Obesity contributes to and may worsen other health problems. It is preventable, yet we often lack the collective will to address it. Still, parents and concerned adults can take steps to help young people make healthier choices so they can lead productive lives rather than becoming statistics.

How did we arrive at this point? Over time, we have become a less physically active society. Many schools have reduced physical education programs. Children spend less time playing outside, partly because parents worry about safety. At the same time, technology has become a dominant part of daily life. Television, computers, video games, and constant digital connection compete for time that once involved movement.

Rather than focusing only on what children eat or how often they move, it is more useful to consider the environments that shape those choices. Health habits rarely fail because children lack information. They falter because the systems surrounding them make unhealthy options easier, louder, and more rewarding in the short term. Influence, therefore, is not simply about correction. It is about design.

Children respond to patterns long before they respond to instruction. What food is available when hunger strikes? What happens after a long school day? Is rest treated as a priority or a luxury? These seemingly small cues send powerful messages about what matters and what can be postponed. Over time, they teach children how to regulate stress, manage fatigue, and seek comfort.

This is where adult influence becomes most effective. Adults do not need to control every choice, but they do need to curate the conditions under which choices are made. A home where fruit is visible and water is accessible communicates something different than one where snacks are hidden behind rules or restriction. A routine that includes movement as a normal part of the day like walking the dog, dancing in the kitchen, stretching before bed, signals that physical activity is not punishment, but part of living.

Health also intersects with emotion. Children learn early which behaviors bring relief when they are tired, frustrated, or overwhelmed. If food becomes the primary coping mechanism, it will be used that way into adulthood. If movement, conversation, rest, or creativity are modeled as options, children expand their internal toolkit for managing stress. Influence, in this sense, is about widening the menu of responses available to them.

When adults approach health as an ongoing practice rather than a set of rules, children are more likely to engage. They begin to associate healthy habits with connection, stability, and care rather than shame or control. This shift does not require perfection. It requires consistency, presence, and an understanding that habits are shaped by what is repeated, not what is explained once.

This becomes clearest when we look at the everyday moments that shape children's expectations.

Healthy eating and exercise do not have to feel like punishment. Creativity matters. Vegetables can be added to familiar meals. Children can help prepare food. Community gardens and shared activities can connect effort, patience, and nutrition in meaningful ways.

Family routines have also changed. With more parents balancing full-time work and caregiving responsibilities, convenience foods and quick meals have become more common. Fast food, highly processed snacks, and packaged meals are often affordable, accessible, and heavily marketed, especially to children. Taken together, these shifts have created environments that make healthy choices harder to sustain and unhealthy patterns easier to adopt. The result has been a steady rise in obesity and related health concerns.

I see this firsthand even in my own family. When I pick up my grandson from school, he is often hungry, and his first request is usually McDonald's. It is not just the food. It is the familiarity, the routine, the promise of something easy and comforting after a long day.

Even with my education and professional experience, I find it difficult to compete with the pull of convenience and branding. If it can be challenging for someone who understands the consequences over time, how much harder must it be for a young, exhausted parent, perhaps juggling multiple jobs or limited resources, to push back against those influences day after day?

So how do we influence children to navigate this perfect storm of trends? We must promote health with the same consistency and creativity that corporations use to promote convenience and indulgence. But we also need to be realistic. Healthy living will never be as easy to sell as pizza or fast food. That means we need a thoughtful plan, and it needs to begin at home.

It is not enough to simply say "no" to children. They are perceptive, curious, and quick to question. If parents, grandparents, and mentors want to influence healthier habits, we must offer alternatives that make sense to children and fit into real life.

Children experience stress, pressure from peers, and emotional ups and downs just like adults do. They need constructive ways to cope with those pressures and to connect health with feeling better, not worse. Regular physical activity plays a powerful role here. Walking, biking, playing, and structured movement support physical health, emotional regulation, and focus. In my experience, many challenges related to attention and restlessness improve when children are more active and consume less sugar, not as a cure all, but as part of a healthier daily rhythm.

Adults have both a responsibility and an opportunity to influence. That influence begins with conversation and presence, spending time talking with children about health, movement, and food in ways they can understand. Just as important, adults must model the behaviors they encourage. Children notice inconsistencies quickly. Healthy habits are far more likely to stick when they are shared and practiced together.

Healthy eating and exercise do not have to feel like punishment. Creativity can make a difference.

- Vegetables may not always be appealing on their own, but adding them to familiar dishes, such as stir-frying carrots and broccoli with protein and seasoning, can make meals more enjoyable.
- If a child enjoys pasta, adding colorful vegetables to the sauce can introduce new foods gradually. Involving children

in washing or preparing ingredients can increase their interest in eating what they helped create.

- Community gardens can offer children the chance to grow food themselves, helping them connect effort, patience, and nutrition in a tangible way.

The same principle applies to physical activity. Children need options. Traditional exercises may feel boring or unsafe in some neighborhoods, but community spaces, such as YMCAs, Boys and Girls Clubs, or organized recreation programs, can provide safe environments where children can move, play, and learn alongside peers.

Beyond individual families, society has a role to play. We need to rethink how institutions support healthy choices. Why is nutritious food still so difficult to find in schools, hospitals, and other settings meant to promote well being? Too often, convenience and cost outweigh health over time. As adults, we must be willing to speak up, ask better questions, and advocate for environments that support healthy habits rather than undermine them.

According to the American Diabetes Association, millions of children and adults in the United States live with diabetes, a condition that carries enormous personal and economic costs. While not all cases are preventable, many could be delayed or managed more effectively through early intervention and healthier lifestyles.

Prevention does not always eliminate illness, but early diagnosis and proactive care are almost always healthier and less costly than waiting for crisis. Unfortunately, our healthcare system often prioritizes treatment of advanced disease over health promotion. It is far easier to pay for emergency interventions than to invest in prevention programs that could reduce suffering and expense in the first place. That approach serves neither individuals nor communities well.

The Interconnectedness of It All

At Edgewater, in our work with individuals who have lived with mental health conditions over time, we often see a complex web of related physical health challenges as well. There is a clear connection between habits such as smoking and conditions like hypertension. In the past, there was a tendency to minimize these concerns, with the belief that certain habits were among the few sources of comfort available. Today, we understand more clearly that supporting people in improving their overall quality of life means helping them address behaviors that affect both mental and physical health.

Encouraging individuals who are managing chronic illness to quit smoking, eat more nutritiously, increase physical activity, and make healthier choices is not simple. Many have heard these messages repeatedly, and resistance or ambivalence is often rooted in stress that has persisted over time, limited support, or the very conditions they are working to manage. Sustainable change requires patience, trust, and consistent encouragement, not just information.

Children who come to us often face even greater challenges. Many struggle with behavioral concerns that interfere with their development into healthy, well-functioning adults. Because their time with us is often brief, they return to environments that may include crowded schools, families under significant stress, and peer groups that exert strong pressure to conform. At times, children may feel excluded because of their behavior. At other times, they may be pulled back toward patterns they are trying to change.

Reaching across that divide to reinforce positive messages around safety, healthy choices, and wellbeing requires persistence and clarity. Supporting children to remain free from violence and substance use is difficult enough, and encouraging healthier eating and activity habits can feel like an additional challenge.

Yet it is not enough to help children break free from cycles of violence or substance use if we do not also support them in developing healthy lifestyles that sustain them over time. Physical health, emotional well-being, and success over time are deeply connected. Children need to understand that habits related to nutrition, movement, and rest play a meaningful role in how they feel, function, and thrive as they grow.

All adults have a responsibility to equip young people with the knowledge and skills needed for a successful life. Success is not defined solely by academic achievement or career attainment. It also includes well-being, balance, and a sense of fulfillment. Those outcomes are far more difficult to achieve without attention to physical health.

Learning healthy habits does not happen in isolation. It is shaped by families, schools, neighborhoods, and communities working together. Without a shared commitment to reinforcing these values, influencing lasting change becomes far more challenging.

As a society, we must continue to advocate for a healthcare system that prioritizes prevention and supports healthy living. At the same time, meaningful change begins at home. Nutritious food, regular movement, and time for rest and connection must be treated as essential components of daily life, not optional ones. Balance between work and personal life is equally important. Constant stress and overwork take a toll on health, while rest and recreation restore energy and resilience.

In my own life, I have learned to be intentional about managing stress by scheduling time for physical activity and leisure just as I would any other important commitment. Whether it is going to the gym, walking, or engaging in simple, enjoyable movement, these practices increase my capacity to be productive and present. The paradox is real. When we make time for health and restoration, we often gain more energy and focus for everything else in our lives.

Taking Healthy Influence to a New Level

As a healthcare leader, I have seen firsthand the cost to our community when health and wellness are treated as secondary concerns rather than foundational priorities. This perspective is shared by most medical professionals who understand that prevention, education, and consistent care are essential to health and wellness.

One such professional is Dr. Steve Simpson, a pediatrician whose lifelong commitment to children and families has made him a trusted presence in Gary, Indiana. Dr. Simpson was raised in Gary and chose to return home after completing his education, not because it was easy, but because he recognized a need. After earning a degree in chemistry and completing medical school and residency, he established his pediatric practice in the community where he grew up, serving families who might otherwise struggle to access consistent, quality care.

Dr. Simpson could have pursued opportunities elsewhere, but instead he chose service. As he puts it simply, "I wanted to come back to Gary to provide healthcare because I knew there was a shortage." For nearly three decades, he has done exactly that, quietly, consistently, and with deep respect for the families he serves.

Parents with limited income, like Diana, are profoundly grateful for his presence. When her daughter, Iyanna, became severely ill at the age of eight, unable to keep food down and rapidly deteriorating, Diana found herself navigating a frightening medical emergency. After being referred to the emergency room and learning her daughter had Type 1 diabetes, she struggled to find immediate specialist care. It was a nurse who offered a practical suggestion: "Get a good pediatrician. He'll know what to do."

Diana knew only one pediatrician, Dr. Simpson. He responded quickly, ran the necessary tests, and then did something just as important. He spoke to her with calm, clarity, and reassurance. "Everything's going to be all right," he told her, before explaining the diagnosis and treatment plan in a way she could understand.

Iyanna is now thriving in her early teens. Her progress reflects not only appropriate medical treatment, but also the lifestyle guidance, education, and ongoing support Dr. Simpson provided to the entire family. He routinely checked in, answered questions, and made himself available beyond scheduled appointments. His care extended beyond symptoms. It addressed the whole child within the context of family and daily life.

Dr. Simpson is quick to deflect praise, often reminding people that he is simply someone who has been fortunate and feels called to give back. Yet his influence is undeniable. He speaks candidly about the challenges he sees daily, missed appointments, delayed vaccinations, and preventable complications, not as evidence of parental failure, but as indicators of systemic stress, limited resources, and gaps in health education.

In any healthcare setting, consistent engagement matters. Preventive care depends on trust, understanding, and follow-through, especially when children's health over time is at stake. Dr. Simpson emphasizes that many health crises could be mitigated through earlier intervention, clearer education, and stronger partnerships between families and providers.

He also raises thoughtful concerns about how we interpret children's behavior. In some cases, behaviors that prompt clinical referrals may reflect environmental stress, limited physical activity, overstimulation, or unmet developmental needs rather than underlying medical conditions. Addressing symptoms without addressing context can lead to incomplete solutions.

Medication can be appropriate and necessary, but it is not a substitute for prevention, structure, nutrition, movement, and adult engagement.

Children benefit most when mental and physical health are considered together, and when adults intervene early, thoughtfully, and with patience.

Dr. Simpson's work reinforces an essential distinction. Medical care treats illness. Preventive influence builds health. Both matter. But lasting outcomes require that we invest more intentionally in the latter, at home, in schools, and throughout our communities.

What We All Can Do to Influence Healthy Habits

Dr. Simpson believes the key to improving the next generation's health begins with education, but not education as we traditionally define it. The three Rs are only a starting point. Children and families also need to understand what health truly means in daily life.

"It's the basics," he explains. "Regular movement. Eating properly. These habits help prevent obesity, diabetes, and hypertension, the same conditions I see every day in adults. And sadly, I'm seeing more of them in children, too."

But education does not happen automatically. Communities that want better outcomes must be willing to invest time, resources, and attention into prevention. Too often, the people who need health education the most lack access to it, while those with knowledge underestimate their responsibility to share it. Progress depends on individuals who are willing to step forward, to advocate, to teach, and to model healthier choices for others.

Dr. Simpson is clear-eyed about the challenges families face. He sees children born into difficult circumstances, including exposure to substance use, instability, and chronic stress from an early age. The substances may change over time, but the underlying vulnerabilities remain. Without early support, these challenges compound. With education and consistent guidance, however, cycles can be interrupted.

Health and education, he emphasizes, are inseparable. Many of the issues he encounters, recurrent illness, school difficulties, and behavioral struggles, can be reduced when families receive better support and information. Teaching children academics alone is not enough. They must also learn how their bodies work, how stress affects them, and how daily choices shape health over time.

Like me, Dr. Simpson believes preparation for adulthood should include preparation for parenting. "Most of us are trained to get jobs," he notes, "but not to raise children. Parenting is learned through trial and error, and families would benefit greatly from understanding early childhood development before problems arise."

He has seen that when parents understand their role more fully, they become more engaged with schools, more connected to their communities, and more confident in guiding their children. That shift, small at first, can influence entire systems over time.

After nearly three decades in pediatric practice, Dr. Simpson's message is simple but powerful. Prevention works. When adults take responsibility for sharing knowledge, modeling healthy habits, and supporting families early, communities grow stronger. By teaching young people the value of personal responsibility and healthy choices now, we begin transforming stress that has persisted over time into opportunities for lasting change.

Health does not exist in isolation. The habits children form around food, movement, rest, and stress shape far more than their bodies. They shape attention, confidence, resilience, and self-trust. When young people are physically depleted, overstimulated, or chronically unwell, their capacity to make sound decisions narrows. What can look like defiance, apathy, or poor judgment is often the result of unmet needs rather than a lack of character.

But when children begin to feel stronger, when their bodies are supported and their routines stabilize, their world widens. They sleep better. They focus longer. They begin to recognize options. Most importantly, they start to believe their choices matter.

This is where influence deepens. Once health creates stability, the next essential task is helping young people learn how to choose, how to pause, assess consequences, and act with intention rather than impulse. That work continues in the next chapter, where we turn our attention to one of the most critical skills a young person can develop, the ability to make sound decisions that align with the life they want to build.

Small Choices, Strong Bodies

Pause and think about what health looked like in the home you grew up in.

What foods were normal?
What movement was modeled?
What did stress look like, and how was it handled?

Now think about the children you influence.

What routines are shaping their bodies and minds?
What habits are being reinforced without anyone naming them?
What is one small choice you could repeat consistently,
so health feels normal rather than forced?

Sit with this truth.
Healthy habits are built quietly, through repetition and example.
A child does not need a perfect plan.
They need a steady one.

Closing Reflection: Influence That Lasts

Healthy habits are not formed overnight, nor are they sustained by lectures, fear, or perfection. They take shape quietly through repetition, encouragement, and example. When children learn to associate health with care, connection, and confidence rather than shame or punishment, they are far more likely to carry those habits into adulthood.

Influencing young people to adopt healthier lives requires patience and persistence. Progress often comes in small steps. Setbacks are part of growth. What matters most is consistency, not intensity, and the willingness to stay engaged even when change feels slow.

Health is more than the absence of illness. It is energy, balance, resilience, and the capacity to participate fully in life. When adults treat well-being as a priority rather than an afterthought, children learn to do the same. They notice what we choose, what we repeat, and what we protect.

As adults, we can influence not only what children know about health, but how they experience it. When we model balance, create supportive environments, and make space for prevention, we give children something more powerful than instructions. We give them a foundation.

Lasting influence does not come from control or perfection. It comes from presence, intention, and care practiced over time. And when those choices are made consistently, they shape futures far beyond what we can see in the moment.

Reflection Question

What everyday habit are you modeling right now, and what message does it send to the young people watching you?

Chapter Five

Influence Youth to Make Sound Decisions

"Sex education, including its spiritual aspects, should be part of a broad health and moral education from kindergarten through grade twelve, ideally carried out harmoniously by parents and teachers."
~ Benjamin Spock, *Dr. Spock's Baby and Child Care*

Every choice carries weight, even when it seems small.

Young people make decisions every day, what to say, who to trust, when to walk away, when to follow, and when to push back. Some choices feel harmless in the moment but echo far beyond it. Others arrive quietly, disguised as convenience or pressure, yet determine direction more than intention alone ever could.

Decision making is not instinctual. It is learned.

As we have seen throughout this book, influence rarely announces itself, but it is always teaching.

Children are not born knowing how to evaluate risk, regulate emotion, or anticipate long term consequences. Those skills develop over time, through guidance, modeling, and practice. When adults assume young people should "just know better," we miss an opportunity to teach what responsibility looks like in real life.

In a world that rewards speed, reaction, and constant stimulation, thoughtful decision making has become harder, not easier, for many young people. Choices are shaped by peers, social media, and the pressure to appear confident even when clarity is missing. Without steady adult influence, many young people learn to decide based on impulse rather than values.

But sound decisions are rarely about intelligence alone. They are shaped by health, environment, emotional safety, and the examples young people observe every day. When children feel supported, grounded, and seen, they are better equipped to pause before acting. They learn that choice is not about control, it is about alignment.

Influencing youth to make sound decisions means more than correcting mistakes after they occur. It requires adults who are willing to slow the moment down, name the options, model accountability, and stay present when outcomes are uncomfortable.

This chapter explores how influence helps young people move from reaction to reflection, and how small moments of guidance can shape lifelong outcomes.

Sex, Safety, and Informed Choices

Sex is a difficult subject for many adults to talk about, yet avoiding it leaves young people vulnerable. Open, age appropriate conversations are among the most effective ways to help youth navigate relationships, protect their health, and avoid consequences they are not prepared to carry.

It used to be that children played outside, yards, sidewalks, neighborhood streets, secure in the belief that staying close to home meant safety. Today, many parents keep kids indoors more often, responding to real concerns in a rapidly changing world. It is a common perception that the world is more dangerous than it was a generation ago.

That is the perception. But is it fully true?

The reality is a complicated mix of new risks, ongoing risks, and progress that still requires vigilance:

- **New risks:** Technology has created new pathways for harm, including online grooming, exploitation, trafficking tactics, and private, unsupervised communication. The same tools that connect and educate can also be used to manipulate and target young people.
- **Ongoing risk:** Many adolescents still engage in sexual activity before they are emotionally or developmentally prepared. Substance use, especially alcohol and drugs, continues to fuel risky decision making by lowering inhibition and impairing judgment.
- **Ongoing risk:** Children and teens face elevated vulnerability in certain contexts because they are still developing and often depend on adults for safety and protection.
- **Ongoing risk:** A significant amount of harm occurs in familiar settings and through known individuals, which makes awareness, early education, and prevention even more essential.
- **Encouraging trend, with context:** Substantiated cases of certain types of child maltreatment declined over time as awareness and prevention efforts improved. However, those gains must be interpreted cautiously. Underreporting and the rise of technology facilitated exploitation mean harm has not disappeared. In many cases, it has changed form.
- **Encouraging opportunity:** Parents and caregivers today are generally more aware of both offline and online risks. That awareness creates an opening for clearer guidance, better boundaries, and more honest conversations.

For better or worse, statistics mean little when you are worried about your own child. Any responsible adult wants to keep children safe. The goal is balance, common sense supervision alongside enough freedom for children to develop independence, confidence, and good judgment. Protecting children from external threats is not enough. They also need guidance, knowledge, and decision making skills for the risks they will inevitably encounter.

Expert Lens: When Silence Becomes Risk

Clinicians consistently observe that young people who lack clear, age-appropriate guidance about sex and relationships are more likely to make decisions rooted in confusion, pressure, or misinformation rather than values or self-respect. When honest conversations are delayed or avoided, curiosity does not disappear. It simply shifts to less reliable sources.

Early, thoughtful dialogue helps young people recognize unhealthy dynamics, understand boundaries, and pause before acting. In practice, prevention is less about fear and more about equipping youth with clarity, language, and the confidence to choose wisely when it matters most.

Silence Is Not Neutral

When adults avoid conversations about sex, values, and boundaries, young people do not stop asking questions. They simply seek answers elsewhere. Silence leaves space for peers, media, and misinformation to fill in the gaps, often without context, care, or concern for consequences over time.

Open, age appropriate dialogue does not encourage risky behavior. It equips young people with clarity, confidence, and the ability to pause before making decisions. When adults speak honestly and listen without judgment, they replace confusion with understanding and fear with trust.

Influence them so we reduce sexually transmitted infections, which can harm health, impair fertility, and create lifelong complications.

Influence them so they can recognize grooming and avoid predators.

Influence them so they can avoid choices that pull them off the path toward healthy relationships, education, and bright futures.

How do we begin? We begin by challenging our discomfort.

Many adults were raised to treat sex as dirty, embarrassing, or off limits. Some carry trauma. Some hold strong spiritual values they want to honor. But whatever your background, sexuality is human. The absence of guidance does not create purity. It creates vulnerability.

If we do not talk about it, our kids will. The only question is who will shape the conversation, and what will they leave out?

Beyond Strangers: Understanding Real Risk

Should we teach children to be cautious with strangers? Of course. But real risk is often more complicated than that.

Small children, especially, are easy to deceive. Even when they are taught to say "no," a stranger who claims, "Your mommy is hurt and asked me to come get you," can still persuade a child to follow.

That reality does not mean children cannot play outside. It means they need layered protection, trusted adults nearby, safe environments, clear check in rules, and age appropriate boundaries.

As children grow older, risks become less visible and more complex. We need to be honest with them about what can happen, not only with strangers, but sometimes with people they know.

Even inside the home, risk does not disappear. Screens, private messaging, and constant exposure to sexualized content create challenges many parents did not face growing up. In an era of more single parent households and demanding work schedules, peer influence can feel louder than parental influence, especially when it comes to sex, substances, late nights, and risky situations.

If we want to protect our children, we have to protect them from their own lack of information. Not by frightening them, but by equipping them. They need enough knowledge to recognize danger, avoid risky situations, and make wiser choices when pressure is applied.

Educate for Influence

The key is for adults to influence our youth, so they do not become victims of preventable consequences, physical, emotional, or relational.

Influence them so they move toward strong futures.

Influence them so we reduce teen pregnancy, which can multiply hardship for young parents and children alike.

Learning to Pause Before Choosing

Take a moment to reflect on how decisions were handled when you were growing up.

What topics were discussed openly?
What topics were avoided?
What did you learn about consequences, boundaries, and self-respect without anyone saying a word?

Now think about the young people in your life.

Do they feel safe asking questions?
Do they know they can pause before deciding?
Do they have language for values, boundaries, and choice?

Sit with this truth.
The ability to pause is a skill.
And skills are learned through presence, patience, and practice.

Closing Reflection

Influence Beyond the Moment

Talking with young people about sex is rarely comfortable, and it is never a single conversation. It is an ongoing exchange shaped by trust, consistency, and presence. What matters most is not having perfect words but being willing to show up repeatedly with honesty and care.

When adults provide accurate information, clear boundaries, and steady guidance, they give young people something essential, the ability to pause, reflect, and choose wisely, especially when no one is watching. Influence works best when it prepares youth not just to avoid harm, but to pursue self-respect, healthy relationships, and futures shaped by intention rather than impulse. Most often, that preparation happens not in lectures, but in small, ordinary moments that quietly shape a young person's internal compass.

Silence is not protection. Avoidance is not guidance. The most powerful gift we can offer is not control over every moment, but a strong internal compass built through truth, consistency, and trust.

Reflection Question

What message about relationships, boundaries, and self-worth are the young people in your life learning from how, and whether, you talk with them about sex?

Chapter Six

Influence Youth to Take Education Seriously

"Education is not preparation for life; education is life itself."
~ John Dewey

Education is central to success in life, and the United States was once an international leader in education. That distinction has become more difficult to sustain. Today, the primary role of education should be to prepare young people to live useful, meaningful lives in the twenty first century. A secondary role is to help our nation remain competitive in an increasingly global economy. Yet in too many American cities, for too long, education has struggled to fully meet either goal.

National education organizations estimate that hundreds of thousands of students disengage from school or leave before graduation each year. Early warning signs, such as chronic absenteeism and course failure, often emerge as early as middle school. Research consistently shows that disengagement from learning is a strong predictor of dropping out.

Political leaders, educators, and parents have made many sincere efforts to reform schools, yet overall performance continues to lag in cities across the nation. Funding alone is not the issue. Some schools achieve remarkable outcomes with limited resources, while others that receive significant investment continue to struggle. This raises an important question: what do students need most to succeed?

Contrary to popular belief, it is not money, resources, or even staffing alone. While all these matter, the deeper issue is commitment. Meaningful change requires shared responsibility. Educators must be committed to preparing students for their futures. Parents must be actively engaged in their children's learning. Communities must genuinely value education as a priority. In short, progress depends on collective influence. Everyone has a role to play in helping young people take education seriously.

The Foundation of Our Community

At first glance, education may appear to concern only schools, students, and parents. In reality, it is a community issue that affects everyone, whether they have school aged children. Today's students will become tomorrow's workforce, leaders, and neighbors. The quality of their education will shape the social and economic health of our communities for generations.

We must ask ourselves: How well is our education system preparing the next generation for work, citizenship, and lifelong learning? How will our communities compete in a global society if students do not develop strong skills, adaptability, and creativity? As industries evolve and technology advances, young people must be prepared to participate in a knowledge based and increasingly specialized workforce.

Public schools must prepare students for a wide range of pathways, including college, business, technical training, and emerging careers. At the same time, schools must attend to students' social and emotional development so they can navigate a complex and rapidly changing world. Failing to do so risks consigning future generations to long term economic and social disadvantage.

Today's children are expected to master far more knowledge than previous generations, often while navigating constant exposure to media that elevates celebrity, material wealth, and spectacle over learning. At a time when expectations should rise, cultural messages can unintentionally lower them. Communities must counter these influences by celebrating curiosity, literacy, innovation, and thoughtful leadership.

The early school years are especially critical. When children fall behind in foundational skills such as reading and math, catching up becomes increasingly difficult. A strong foundation equips students to engage confidently with new technologies and future learning demands.

Students must master both the basics and emerging tools, reading, writing, and mathematics alongside digital literacy and global communication. The world is changing rapidly, requiring greater flexibility and critical thinking from young adults. Meeting these demands will require fresh ideas, sustained investment, and a willingness for education systems to adapt.

Technology can be a powerful ally in learning. When used thoughtfully, digital tools can engage students, support creativity, and enhance research and communication skills. At the same time, schools must continue to insist on strong literacy, numeracy, and analytical skills. These remain essential across all fields and disciplines.

Ultimately, education is about learning how to think. There are no shortcuts to developing critical thinking and a love of learning. Individuals who cultivate curiosity and adaptability throughout life are better prepared to navigate change, while those who never develop these habits often face unnecessary struggle.

Fix What's Broken

Improvement begins with honest evaluation, identifying what works and what does not, both locally and nationally. With thousands of school districts operating independently, successful innovations are not always shared, while ineffective programs may persist longer than they should.

Effective practices should be evaluated, refined, and shared. Programs that no longer meet current needs should be thoughtfully retired. Teachers who develop successful approaches deserve tangible support and recognition. When classrooms struggle, educators should receive guidance, professional development, and meaningful support. If challenges persist despite intervention, difficult personnel decisions may be necessary in the best interest of students.

Many talented, dedicated teachers remain deeply committed to their work, yet they often feel isolated within systems that do not fully support innovation. Increasing behavioral challenges, evolving discipline policies, and limited resources can undermine even the best instructional plans.

As discipline approaches have changed, educators often have fewer tools to address persistent disruptions. In response, schools may rely more heavily on exclusionary practices such as suspension or expulsion. While sometimes necessary, these measures can unintentionally remove students from the very environments that provide structure and support.

Removing a struggling student from school without addressing underlying needs often produces the opposite of the intended result. When students are excluded without adequate support, they may spend more time unsupervised, increasing exposure to negative influences and reinforcing harmful patterns.

Many classroom challenges reflect broader issues beyond school walls, including food insecurity, housing instability, or inconsistent caregiving. While families bear primary responsibility for meeting children's needs, schools inevitably feel the impact when those needs go unmet. Effective education requires flexibility, compassion, and a broader vision of student support.

Schools can help interrupt cycles of instability by serving as connectors, linking families to counselors, health care providers, social services, and mentoring programs. In this way, schools become community hubs that strengthen the foundation for learning and long-term success.

The Influence of Parents and Community

Education Is a Daily Practice

Education does not begin at the schoolhouse door, nor does it end when the final bell rings. Every conversation, expectation, and example shapes what children believe about learning, whether it matters, whether it is attainable, and whether it belongs to them. When adults model curiosity, accountability, and engagement, education becomes not just a requirement, but a way of life.

Parents and caregivers play a critical role in shaping children's attitudes toward learning. When adults demonstrate curiosity, persistence, and respect for education, young people are more likely to internalize those values. Education is reinforced through everyday experiences, reading together, discussing current events, and exploring the world beyond immediate surroundings.

Many families face real pressures, including long work hours and financial strain. Educators, too, often operate within systems stretched thin. Sustainable improvement requires partnership rather than blame. Progress emerges through shared accountability and daily choices made in homes, classrooms, and communities.

Businesses and local organizations also have a role to play. Partnerships that offer mentorship, internships, and exposure to real world applications help students see how education connects to future opportunities. When learning feels purposeful, students are more likely to stay engaged and persist.

Influence in Action

To illustrate the power of timely influence, consider a firefighter I know, we will call him Sam, who helped redirect a young person's educational path.

During a quiet winter day, Sam and a colleague visited a local fitness center. Two teenage boys arrived, and the group decided to play a game of basketball. After some lighthearted competitive banter, Sam noticed that one of the teens, JC, showed remarkable athletic ability.

When Sam asked about school, JC shared that he had left due to family responsibilities and instability at home. Sam challenged him to think about whether his circumstances would define his future. Over time, Sam built trust, encouraged JC to return to school, and helped him reconnect with education through basketball.

Although setbacks followed, including eligibility and academic hurdles, Sam continued to support JC. With guidance and persistence, JC earned a GED, attended junior college, and eventually received a scholarship to a university. Today, he is self sufficient and thriving, a powerful example of how consistent adult influence can change a life's trajectory.

Sam's impact came from meeting JC where he was, understanding his circumstances, and connecting education to something meaningful. Influence, when applied thoughtfully and persistently, can reignite purpose and possibility.

Embrace the Future

As we evaluate education, we should avoid becoming overly dependent on numbers alone. While data matters, it must be paired with deeper questions about curriculum relevance, resources, parental engagement, and student support.

Families and communities must become informed partners, asking questions, celebrating success, and advocating for systems that support both students and educators. Improvement does not require reinventing education from scratch. It begins by identifying effective teachers, programs, and schools and learning from what already works.

The world is changing rapidly. To prepare future leaders, education must evolve with curiosity, courage, and collaboration. When communities invest in learning through consistency, care, and shared responsibility, young people gain the tools they need to succeed.

The Space Between Impulse and Choice

Pause for a moment and consider a decision you made when you were young that shaped your life in ways you did not fully understand at the time.

What influenced that decision?
Who was present, and who was absent?
What information did you have, and what was missing?

Now consider the young people in your life today.

Are they being rushed to decide without reflection?
Are they absorbing messages without guidance?
Do they know that pausing is not weakness, but wisdom?

Breathe here.

Influence does not remove choice.
It strengthens it.

The goal is not control, but clarity.
Not fear, but understanding.
Not silence, but steady presence.

Every pause you model becomes permission for a young person to think before acting.

Closing Reflection

Education flourishes where belief meets consistency. Schools cannot do this work alone, and families cannot shoulder it in isolation. When communities align around the shared responsibility of learning, young people gain more than knowledge. They gain direction, confidence, and opportunity.

Reflection Question

Learning now happens everywhere, in classrooms, homes, and digital spaces. What does your daily behavior teach the young people around you about the value of education?

Chapter Seven

Influence Youth in a Digital World

"The smallest click can steer the largest consequences, but awareness can reclaim the wheel."
~ Dr. Danita Johnson Woods

Education taught us what to learn. Now we examine who is shaping how we learn.

Before we talk about screens, apps, or algorithms, we need to talk about influence.

Today's young people are growing up in a world where guidance does not always come from the adults in their lives. It comes from digital systems designed to capture attention, shape preferences, and quietly reinforce beliefs. Parents, caregivers, educators, and mentors can no longer afford to be passive observers of this reality. To influence youth in a digital world, we must first understand how influence operates there and then help young people recognize when their choices are being guided without their awareness.

We live in a time when what young people see, believe, and even feel is often shaped by forces they barely notice.

Influence no longer comes only from parents, teachers, or peers. It comes quietly, through algorithms designed to capture attention, amplify emotion, and reinforce patterns of thought. These systems do not shout or demand. They hum, subtly and persistently, guiding choices one scroll, one click, one suggested video at a time.

This chapter is about learning to hear that hum.

Because freedom in the digital age is not just the ability to choose. It is the ability to recognize when the power to choose is slowly being redirected.

The Algorithm and Me: Javier's Aha Moment

Through Javier's story, we see how small, unnoticed shifts in a digital life can shape much larger shifts in real life, and how awareness, reclaimed one decision at a time, can restore agency, clarity, and direction.

The digital world may shape the feed.

But influence, and the future, still belong to us.

The Narrowing Feed

This is my story.

I'm Javier Cardona, Black, Puerto Rican, and stubborn from birth, raised by a single mother who believed deeply in civic responsibility. My mom paid attention to the world. She watched debates, read the news, and made sure I understood why history mattered, even when I rolled my eyes.

When I was fifteen, though, my attention drifted elsewhere.

It started harmlessly enough, short clips, viral debates, confident voices offering sharp answers. The algorithm noticed what held my attention and offered more of the same.

Slowly, my feed narrowed.

What I didn't realize at the time was how quietly it was happening. One day, I started feeling a certain way about issues I hadn't really thought deeply about before. Another day, I felt irritated, almost defensive, about perspectives I once understood or even agreed with. I didn't stop to ask myself where those reactions were coming from.

I assumed they were mine.

But they weren't fully.

News outlets I once trusted began to feel biased. Ads seemed to echo my fears before I could even articulate them. I wasn't just searching for information anymore. It was finding me.

And shaping me.

The Wake Up Call

During a local election season, something shifted.

Scrolling through my phone, I noticed that nearly everything I saw supported the same narrative. The other side was always framed as foolish, dangerous, or dishonest. It became easy to believe what I was being shown, even when it conflicted with my lived experiences, or with the values my mother had spent years instilling in me.

That's when I paused.

Not dramatically. Just long enough to ask myself a quiet question.

When did I stop questioning what I was being fed?

I realized I had been influenced without noticing it at first. Certain content had nudged my emotions, my anger, my certainty, my sense of belonging, without ever asking me to slow down and think.

And that's when it hit me.

I couldn't vote for vibes. I had to vote for reality.

In 2024, I voted for the first time. Standing in that booth, I wasn't thinking about headlines or trending clips. I was thinking about my mom, my community, and the kind of future I wanted to help shape.

I couldn't afford to be passive anymore.

Choosing a Different Path

Taking control of my narrative meant more than unfollowing accounts.

It meant paying attention to how content made me feel.

It meant asking why certain messages stirred fear or outrage so easily.

It meant noticing whose voices were missing from my feed, and why.

I started expanding what I consumed, intentionally. I followed creators who looked like me. I listened to people who disagreed with me but didn't mock or dehumanize others. I began questioning the easy answers I had once clung to.

Some days, it felt uncomfortable. Other days, it felt freeing.

In that process, I realized something important. I wasn't just a consumer of information. I was a participant in shaping my worldview.

That realization changed everything.

Don't Argue the Opinion, Question the Input

When conversations with young people turn tense or defensive, it's tempting to argue conclusions. But in a digital world, the more productive question is not "Why do you think that?" It's "Where did that idea come from?"

Algorithms shape beliefs long before opinions are fully formed. Teaching young people to examine their inputs, what they watch, who they follow, which voices are amplified, and which are absent, helps them reclaim agency without feeling controlled. Influence grows strongest not when adults dictate what to believe, but when they help young people slow down, notice patterns, and ask better questions about what's shaping their thinking.

The Ripple Effect

Looking back, I can see how many conversations were strained by information I never fact checked. How many relationships, especially with my mom, were tested because we were living in different digital realities.

The algorithm hadn't just influenced what I believed.

It had shaped who I trusted.

It also took a toll on my mental health. Spending time in spaces where people joked about harm, dismissed entire communities, or treated cruelty as humor left marks I didn't immediately recognize.

At some point, I asked myself another quiet question.

If something as small as a click can pull people apart, could a conscious choice begin to pull them back together?

I believe it can.

Our digital lives spill into our real ones, into family conversations, classrooms, elections, and dreams. Choosing differently online becomes an act of care offline.

Freedom isn't something you fight for all at once.

It's something you reclaim, detail by detail.

Javier's Reflection

Now I'm older, in my early twenties.

I still question things.

I still stay skeptical.

But I also stay open.

I check sources.

I listen to people who challenge me.

I notice when content is trying to provoke rather than inform.

I don't let the algorithm decide who I become.

I choose.

Practical Influence: A Digital Discernment Toolkit

Influencing youth in a digital world does not require mastering every platform or trend. It begins with helping young people notice what is shaping them. Encourage them to pay attention to patterns, what shows up repeatedly in their feed, what emotions it triggers, and what ideas feel familiar simply because they are repeated.

Teach the pause before reaction.

Why does this make me feel this way?

Who benefits if I believe it?

What might be missing from this picture?

Model discernment together by checking sources, reading beyond headlines, and comparing perspectives that inform rather than inflame. Help young people widen their digital world intentionally, following voices that educate, challenge respectfully, and reflect diverse lived experiences. And remind them that stepping away is also a choice.

The goal is not to control information, but to cultivate an internal compass strong enough to navigate, one thoughtful decision at a time.

The Space Between Scroll and Self

Pause for a moment and consider how often your attention is guided without invitation.

What content do you return to automatically?
What emotions rise most quickly when you scroll?
What voices shape your thinking without being named?

Now think about the young people watching you.
Do they see you pause before reacting?
Do they see you question sources instead of repeating them?
Do they know that choosing differently is allowed?

Breathe here.

Awareness is not resistance.
It is reclamation.
Each pause creates space for choice.
Each choice restores agency.
What you notice, you can change.

Closing Reflection

The Quiet Power of Awareness

In a world driven by speed, noise, and digital persuasion, real influence begins with awareness.

The smallest habits, the posts we linger on, the voices we amplify, the ideas we accept without question, quietly shape who young people are becoming. Over time, those small choices accumulate, forming beliefs, identities, and futures.

Javier's story reminds us that influence rarely announces itself. More often, it works silently, through repetition and familiarity, until young people stop noticing where their thoughts originated.

Adults cannot control every message youth encounter. But we can teach them how to pause, question, and choose with intention. We can model curiosity instead of certainty, discernment instead of reaction, and courage instead of conformity.

Because in the end, it is not the loudest voices or the most persuasive feeds that shape a life.

It is the quiet, consistent practice of thinking critically.
Of listening carefully.
Of choosing wisely, one small decision at a time.

Reflection Question

How often do you help the young people in your life slow down long enough to notice who, or what, is influencing them?

Chapter Eight

Influence Youth to Stop Violence

"Violence is learned—and so is peace."
~ Dr. Danita Johnson Woods

Our children have not disappeared, but many have become unheard.

We didn't lose them overnight. The disconnect happened gradually, quietly, and often unintentionally. It wasn't caused by the spread of drugs in our communities. That was a symptom. It wasn't caused by metal detectors in schools, that was a response. It wasn't caused by violent media alone—that reflected deeper fractures already present.

The real turning point came when adults stopped listening—when we confused exposure with maturity and urgency with readiness.

Too often, we expect children to navigate adult realities without adult support. We speak to them as if they are fully formed, emotionally equipped decision-makers, forgetting that childhood is meant to be a protected season of learning, testing, and growth. Children need room to make mistakes—but also boundaries strong enough to keep those mistakes from becoming life-altering.

When we rush children into adulthood, we don't strengthen them, we burden them.

Let Kids Be Kids

Because the world feels more dangerous, many adults respond by either overexposing children to harsh realities or shielding them entirely. Neither approach serves them well.

Children need guidance that is honest but age-appropriate, preparation without panic, truth without fear. When we overwhelm children with adult problems before they are ready to process them, we risk undermining the very developmental foundation they need to thrive later.

We cannot return to an earlier era, nor should we pretend the risks are unchanged. Today's children are growing up in a world of rapid change, expanded access, and constant stimulation. That reality demands more intentional leadership from adults, not less.

As parents, educators, mentors, and community members, our role remains clear: we lead, so children can learn how to follow safely before they are expected to lead themselves.

Children, especially adolescents, test limits. That is not defiance; it is development.

Our responsibility is not to eliminate risk entirely, but to introduce responsibility gradually, widening boundaries only when readiness is demonstrated. When adults step back too early, children are left to learn critical lessons through consequences that can be irreversible.

Childhood is a training ground, not a battlefield.

If we want to influence young people away from violence and toward healthier choices, we must be intentional about how we guide them—starting early, staying consistent, and leading by example.

Three Foundations for Prevention

1. Prepare Children Gradually

Introduce adult realities in stages. Just as we would never expect a student to master advanced mathematics without first learning the basics, we cannot expect children to navigate peer pressure, substance exposure, or conflict without years of guided learning.

Conversations about safety, violence, and decision-making should begin early, at developmentally appropriate levels, and continue consistently. Waiting for the "right time" often means waiting too long.

2. Lead With Clarity, Not Fear

Children need adults who are willing to lead, not withdraw authority out of discomfort or fear of being disliked.

Being a trusted adult does not require being permissive. Clear expectations, consistent consequences, and dependable follow-through create safety, even when children resist in the moment. Respect is built through structure.

3. Model What You Hope to Teach

Children learn more from what they observe than from what they are told.

Homes and communities marked by instability, unresolved conflict, or harmful coping patterns can unintentionally pass those patterns forward—unless someone interrupts the cycle. Awareness is the first step. Support is the second. Change is possible, but it requires adults to seek help when needed and extend grace when guiding others.

Community-based programs, such as structured sports leagues, mentorship initiatives, and supervised evening activities—have demonstrated the power of positive influence during high-risk hours. When young people are given structure, accountability, and a sense of belonging, behavior often shifts—not because of punishment, but because of connection.

Adults who choose engagement over exclusion often become the turning point in a young person's story.

Violence Begins Long Before the Act

Violence rarely starts with a weapon.
It starts with disconnection.

It grows when children feel unseen, unheard, or unprotected.
When anger replaces language.
When fear goes unacknowledged.
When boundaries disappear, or arrive only as punishment.

Most young people who act violently are not driven by cruelty. They are driven by confusion, pain, and a lack of tools to manage overwhelming emotion.

Prevention begins early, long before crisis.
It begins with adults who listen closely.
Who set limits with care.
Who model how to handle conflict without harm.

When adults stay present, even when it is uncomfortable, violence loses its grip.

Influence in Action: When One Adult Shows Up

A close friend once shared his experience mentoring a young man whose life could have gone in a very different direction.

The young man, whom I'll call Eric, grew up in a neighborhood marked by economic hardship and limited adult supervision. He lived in a single-parent household where his mother, stretched thin, struggled to provide consistent guidance. By the time Eric was twelve, he had become loosely involved with peers engaged in risky and illegal activity.

School attendance became sporadic, minor offenses followed, and before long he spent more time on the streets than in classrooms.

At sixteen, Eric showed up one night at a community midnight basketball league, an initiative designed to provide structured activity during the hours when youth are most vulnerable to negative influences. Although he was younger than the program's target age, the organizer made a deliberate choice to let him stay.

At first, Eric tested every boundary. He was loud, dismissive of authority, and quick to challenge rules. Beneath that bravado, however, was a young person hungry for attention, structure, and someone who cared enough to expect more of him.

Rather than pushing him out, the organizer chose engagement over exclusion. He spent time getting to know Eric , asking questions, listening carefully, and setting clear expectations. Participation came with conditions: respectful behavior, accountability, and responsibility both on and off the court.

Over time, something shifted.

Eric began showing up consistently. His behavior improved. He distanced himself from negative influences and returned to school more regularly. The structure, combined with consistent adult presence, created space for him to imagine a different future.

Years later, Eric is gainfully employed and a small business partner. His life is not perfect, but it is stable, purposeful, and far removed from the path he once seemed destined to follow.

Eric's story is not about sports or second chances alone. It is about what happens when an adult refuses to give up, sets firm boundaries, and offers guidance rooted in respect rather than fear. It is proof that influence does not require extraordinary resources—only presence, consistency, and belief.

Preventing violence is rarely about punishment. It is about presence, protection, and adults willing to intervene before harm becomes identity.

When One Adult Changes the Outcome

Influence doesn't always arrive in the form of programs or policies.

Sometimes it shows up as one adult who notices, stays, and refuses to walk away.

Pause and consider:

- Who showed up for you when you were testing limits?
- Who might be waiting for that kind of presence from you now?

When Good Turns Risky

Just as digital spaces can shape behavior without supervision, real-world environments do the same when guidance and boundaries are absent.

Sometimes, despite our best efforts, a child veers toward unhealthy or risky behavior. This does not mean their future is lost. The key is early awareness and timely adjustment—shifting how we influence, support, and guide them back on course.

Helpful practices include:

- Maintaining predictable routines for sleep, meals, and activities
- Encouraging involvement in structured programs that foster accountability and belonging
- Communicating openly and consistently, choosing moments when conversations can be calm and constructive
- Inviting dialogue rather than issuing commands, while maintaining clear limits and consequences

Setting boundaries early, and holding them consistently, helps children understand that expectations matter. Discipline, when grounded in care and consistency, becomes a tool for protection rather than control.

Ultimately, children learn what they live. When they experience chaos, neglect, or violence, those patterns can take root. When they experience structure, care, and kindness, those lessons take hold instead.

Children do not disappear when adults stay engaged.

An Inside Perspective

A longtime law enforcement professional in Indiana shared insights from decades of working with youth impacted by violence and community instability. His experience, both growing up in urban environments and later working in violent crime prevention, underscored a consistent truth: children who are denied childhood often carry that loss into adulthood.

He described how, in some communities, young people are drawn into criminal networks not solely by coercion, but by attention, resources, and a sense of belonging absent elsewhere. When systems fail to offer consistent guidance, harmful alternatives step in.

Yet even in these realities, he emphasized that early intervention, strong school engagement, and honest communication between adults and children can make a difference. Schools, families, and communities function best when expectations are aligned and support is consistent.

His advice to parents was simple and enduring: know your children, stay involved, set clear expectations, and talk openly about difficult topics. When adults lead with respect, honesty, and consistency, young people are far more likely to respond in kind.

Soul Pause

The Moment Before It Escalates

Pause for a moment and think about a time you felt anger rise quickly, before you had words for it.

What did your body feel first?
Where did the tension land?
What did you truly need in that moment—safety, respect, reassurance, or simply to be heard?

Now think about the young people in your world.

How often are they carrying adult stress in child-sized bodies?
How often are they expected to "handle it" without being taught how?
How often do they act out what they cannot yet explain?

Breathe here.

Peace is not passive.
It is practiced.

It looks like slowing the moment down.
It looks like boundaries that protect, not punish.
It looks like an adult who stays present long enough for a child to come back to themselves.

Ask yourself:

Where can I model the pause before the reaction?
Where can I lead with clarity, not fear?
Where can I be the steady voice that keeps a hard moment from becoming a hard life?

Closing Reflection

Violence does not begin with a weapon—it begins with absence.

Absence of listening.

Absence of boundaries.

Absence of adults willing to stay present when a child is confused, angry, or searching for belonging.

When children are guided with consistency, protected with intention, and seen as worthy of patience rather than punishment, cycles of violence can be interrupted. Influence, applied early and steadily, does more than correct behavior, it preserves childhood and creates space for healthier futures.

Reflection Question

Who is listening closely enough to the children in your world—and if no one is, will you be the one who does?

Chapter Nine

Influence Youth to Rise Above Failure

"Failure is the foundation of success, and the means by which it is achieved."
~ Lao Tzu

Failure is part of being human. Every one of us will stumble at some point, often more than once. What matters most is not whether failure occurs, but whether we learn how to respond when it does. Resilience, not perfection, is the foundation of lasting success.

Young people learn how to handle failure by watching the adults in their lives. When we model perseverance, when we show that setbacks are not endings but redirections, we give them permission to try again. In that sense, rising after failure is not only a personal responsibility, but also a communal one. We owe it to ourselves, our communities, and the next generation to demonstrate what recovery, growth, and determination look like in real life.

Encouraging youth to succeed does not mean shielding them from disappointment. It means helping them develop the confidence and internal stability to face challenges without losing belief in themselves. Success, especially for young people, is deeply tied to whether they feel capable and supported in the present, not just measured against future outcomes.

- Celebrate your child's accomplishments.
  There's always a reason to celebrate with children. Acknowledging their progress in genuine, open, and joyful ways helps them feel capable. When you, or another significant person in their life, affirms their unique talents, skills, and gifts, their internal "success barometer" rises.
- Accept your child as they are today.
  It is vital to accept children for who they are, not only for who we hope they will become. Wanting the best for your child is natural, but don't let that desire turn into disappointment when they fall short (in your opinion). Children are tuned in quickly when they are not meeting expectations, and that can affect motivation and self-esteem.
- Give your child's talent time to develop.
  Comparison starts early, sometimes as early as the first doctor's report of weight and length. But not all children develop on the same timeline physically, mentally, or emotionally. Support and encourage your child at every stage of growth, and watch their confidence expand over time.

Instead of framing feedback in ways that unintentionally diminish effort, we can affirm progress while still encouraging growth. A child who brings home a B average may hear very different messages depending on how adults respond. For some, encouragement fuels motivation. For others, even well intended pressure can lead to discouragement or disengagement.

The goal is not to lower expectations, but to pair them with acceptance. When children feel valued for who they are today, they are more willing to stretch toward who they are becoming.

When Failure Feels Personal

Failure can feel like a label instead of a lesson, especially for young people who already doubt themselves. Some children carry disappointment quietly. Others mask it with anger, humor, or withdrawal. The adult response matters. When we treat failure as information, not identity, we teach children that setbacks are survivable and that effort still counts. Encouragement does not erase accountability; it supports the courage it takes to try again.

The Three Ps for Success

Even with our best efforts, failures will occur. They're inevitable. But failure never means everything is lost.

Sometimes overcoming failure requires reshaping priorities. You are never "a failure at life" because you made mistakes that forced you to change course. In fact, turning setbacks into insight is an essential ingredient in any success story. The task is not insurmountable. If you can envision change, you can begin to make change.

Often, failures teach us lessons that success cannot. Sometimes we only learn what not to do before we see clearly what we must do.

Unfortunately, we live in a culture that often expects instant results, quick wins, fast recognition, and overnight success. That belief can create an "all or nothing" mindset. Either you succeed, or you fail, no in between. But there is an in between. The stretch of time where growth is happening, even if results are not visible yet.

Let me share a story that illustrates how failure does not have to be final.

When Failure Isn't the End of the Story

Patty grew up in a home marked by instability and limited support. By middle school, she was already struggling, acting out, encountering the legal system, and drifting further from school. At sixteen, she left high school altogether and became entangled in substance use. Over time, addiction narrowed her choices and placed both her health and future at risk. She became a mother twice during this period but was not in a position to care for her children, who were lovingly raised by her sister.

Change did not come quickly. For nearly two decades, Patty remained stuck in patterns that reinforced struggle rather than possibility. Her turning point came after an arrest for shoplifting, an experience that forced her to pause and confront the direction of her life. While incarcerated, she had time to reflect, and for the first time, she made a deliberate decision to pursue recovery and stability.

After her release, Patty began rebuilding step by step. She attended recovery meetings, found work, and reconnected with her children. She returned to high school as an adult learner, at one point attending classes alongside her own son, and eventually earned her diploma. Progress was slow and demanding, but it was steady.

As her confidence grew, so did her vision. Patty continued her education, earning both a bachelor's and a master's degree. Today, she is pursuing a Ph.D. in counseling, using her lived experience to support others, navigating their own path forward.

Patty's story is not typical, and it is not meant to be. It is extreme. But it makes one truth unmistakably clear. Failure does not define a life. Persistence does. And if transformation is possible after years of setbacks, then growth is possible at any point, for any of us.

Patty's journey reflects the quiet strength of the Three Ps in action. She rediscovered passion by imagining a future different from her past. She shifted her perspective from survival to possibility. And through steady perseverance, she moved forward one decision at a time. Nothing about her transformation was instant, but each small, intentional step built momentum toward lasting change.

Where might perseverance, not perfection, be the missing ingredient in how you or the young people you influence define success?

When perseverance gives us the courage to begin again, goals give us a way to move forward with intention instead of guesswork.

To help youth navigate the space between failure and success, keep the Three Ps in mind:

Passion

What captures your attention? What activities make time pass quickly or spark curiosity and energy? Passion doesn't always announce itself loudly, sometimes it reveals itself quietly through interests that return again and again over time. If you're unsure what your passion is, looking back can be a helpful starting point. What did you enjoy before expectations or responsibilities narrowed your choices?

The same is true for children. Passions often emerge gradually and imperfectly. A child may be drawn to art, music, math, writing, sports, science, technology, or to interests adults don't immediately recognize as valuable. What matters most is not whether we understand the interest, but whether we are willing to explore what it might become.

An interest that appears "frivolous" on the surface can become the seed of something meaningful. Curiosity about video games, for example, can evolve into skills in design, programming, problem solving, storytelling, or digital innovation. When adults take time to understand what draws a child in, they create space for growth rather than discouragement.

The role of influence is not to dictate passion, but to nurture it, helping young people see possibilities within their interests and encouraging them to develop those interests with purpose, discipline, and confidence.

Positive Perspective

How we interpret our circumstances often matters as much as the circumstances themselves. When life doesn't unfold as planned, and it rarely does, the question becomes: do we allow disappointment to define the moment, or do we use it as information that guides our next step? Conditions may be imperfect or unfair, but our internal perspective can determine whether those conditions become barriers or turning points.

Perspective is not denial. It is not pretending setbacks don't hurt. It is choosing how we respond once they appear. Young people learn this not from lectures, but from observation. When adults model resilience, acknowledging challenges while refusing to be defeated by them, children learn that struggle and progress can coexist.

Sharing your own experiences with setbacks, uncertainty, or redirection can be especially powerful. When children hear how you reframed disappointment or learned from failure, they see that perspective is something that can be developed over time, not a trait reserved for the naturally optimistic.

Learning to focus on what can be learned, changed, or improved is a habit. Like any habit, it grows with practice. By helping children recognize that a difficult moment does not define their future, we equip them with a mindset that supports perseverance, confidence, and long-term growth.

Perseverance

Most meaningful success unfolds over time. Setbacks, delays, and detours are not signs that something has gone wrong, they are part of the process. Perseverance is the ability to continue moving forward even when progress feels slow or uncertain, and it is one of the most important qualities we can help young people develop.

Children will encounter obstacles. They will fail tests, miss opportunities, fall short of expectations, and sometimes lose confidence. What matters most is not the setback, but what they learn from it. Perseverance teaches that effort is not wasted simply because results are delayed. It reinforces the truth that growth often requires multiple attempts, and that persistence, not perfection, leads to progress.

Adults shape this mindset. When we normalize struggle and emphasize consistency over instant results, we help children understand that success is built through small, repeated actions. Sharing examples of goals that took time, whether in education, career, health, or personal growth, reinforces endurance as strength, not flaw.

Perseverance also teaches patience with oneself. In a culture that celebrates quick wins, young people need reminders that real achievement is rarely immediate. Learning to stay engaged, adjust strategies, and keep going, especially when motivation fades, is a skill that serves them far beyond childhood.

When passion gives direction, perspective provides balance, and perseverance sustains effort, the natural next step is helping young people turn those qualities into clear, achievable goals.

Find Success with Goals

One of the most practical ways to help young people rise above failure is to guide them in setting meaningful goals. Goals give direction to effort. They transform hope into intention and intention into action. When children learn how to set goals, they begin to understand that progress is something they can shape rather than something they wait for.

Before introducing any framework, pause to ask:

What is one thing you want to improve, learn, or change, and what would it feel like to take the first small step toward it?

Goal setting is not about pressure or perfection. It is about helping young people imagine possibilities and move toward them with purpose. The good news is that goal setting is a learned skill, and it can be taught in simple, age appropriate ways.

Here is a straightforward approach that helps children turn ideas into action:

1. What is a goal?
   A goal completes the sentence: "I want to…" Goals give shape to dreams by naming them clearly.

2. Why is setting a goal important?
   Goals help us see what is possible. They give us something to work toward and a reason to stay engaged, even when progress feels slow.

3. How do I know a goal is a good one?
   A strong goal describes what you want, when you want it, and why it matters to you.
   Example: "I want to move to the next reading level by my birthday because I want to feel more confident in class."

4. How do I achieve my goal?
   Create a plan. Picture your goal at the top of a ladder. Each rung is a small step. You don't climb the whole ladder at once, you climb one rung at a time.

5. What if I don't reach my goal right away?
   That's part of learning. Missed goals are opportunities to reflect, adjust, and try again. The lesson isn't perfection, it's persistence.

As you help children set goals, support their efforts without taking control. Let them choose goals that matter to them and take ownership of their plan. When young people feel responsible for their goals, they are more likely to follow through, and more likely to see themselves as capable.

Teaching children how to set and pursue goals equips them with a life skill that extends far beyond school. Influence is strongest when it is lived, not just taught.

A Foundation for Life

I believe growing up with limited resources helped prepare me for the challenges I would later face as a single, working mother pursuing an education. As children, we learned how to make do. As an adult, I drew on that same resilience, along with the steady encouragement of my mother and grandmother, who consistently told me, “You can do anything you put your mind to.” Over time, I learned the deeper truth behind that saying: belief matters, but action is what turns belief into change.

Going to college with a young child was difficult. When I started, I worried I would not belong. Instead, I found a diverse community of learners, people of many ages and backgrounds, reminding me that growth is not limited to one stage of life.

Balancing motherhood, work, and school forced me to develop discipline. Managing limited finances taught me responsibility. What initially felt like obstacles became training grounds for skills that would later serve me well. Progress was not easy or fast, but it was steady.

I also benefited from the guidance of others: a cousin who had already navigated college, supportive counselors, and an academic leader who saw potential in me before I fully saw it myself. Their encouragement reinforced an essential truth; success is rarely a solo journey.

There were also voices that tried to undermine my confidence by tying my future to my past. I learned that not every opinion deserves space in your mind. Some people project their own fears onto others, mistaking ambition for arrogance or growth for betrayal. Guarding your belief in yourself is not selfish, it is necessary.

My grandmother often said, "Don't make other people's problems your problems. If they can't deal with the fact that you are moving forward, keep moving anyway." Her words continue to steady me. They remind me that progress requires courage, especially when growth makes others uncomfortable.

Earning my bachelor's degree was a milestone, not just academically, but personally. It affirmed something I had slowly come to understand; failure does not cancel potential. It clarifies it. Step by step, I learned that I could reshape my life at any point by choosing not to give up.

"Never give up" sounds dramatic, but in practice, it is a daily decision. Real change happens one day at a time. Small goals, taken seriously, create momentum. In a culture that prizes instant results, persistence often feels unremarkable, but it is the quiet engine behind lasting success.

Choose Success

Whatever success looks like for your child, help them understand that meaningful growth takes time. Progress is rarely linear, and setbacks do not signal defeat. At the same time, don't allow children to underestimate themselves. They should not let others define their worth, or allow failure to do so, except as a lesson that informs their next step.

Influence youth to keep going when effort doesn't immediately pay off. They will encounter disappointment. That is unavoidable. What matters is how they respond. A setback can become a stopping point, or a turning point, depending on the guidance they receive.

This is where your influence matters most. Show young people that failure is survivable. That criticism does not erase value. That trying again is not weakness, but courage. Teach them to reflect rather than retreat, to adjust rather than abandon, and to move forward with greater awareness.

Encourage responsibility without shame. Help children identify what went wrong, take ownership where appropriate, repair what they can, and apply what they've learned. Growth happens when accountability is paired with compassion.

The choice is not between perfection and defeat. The real choice is whether to learn and continue, or to stop trying. Success is built through consistent effort, guided reflection, and the willingness to begin again.

You don't need certainty to move forward, only commitment. Choose progress. Choose growth. And keep taking the next right step, even when the path unfolds slowly.

The Courage to Begin Again

Pause for a moment and think about a time you failed,
or fell short, in a way that stayed with you.

What did you believe about yourself afterward?
What did you say to yourself in private?
Who helped you stand back up, and who made it harder?

Now bring to mind a young person you influence.

If they failed today, what would they assume it means?
Would they see it as a verdict, or as feedback?

Would they know they are still worthy of effort, growth, and another try?

Breathe here.

Failure is a moment.
It is not a name.

And the most powerful influence you offer is not a life without setbacks,it is the example of how to rise, with humility, courage, and consistency.

Closing Reflection

Failure is not a verdict, it is feedback. Every stumble carries information, and every detour holds the potential for direction. When young people learn that falling short does not disqualify them from moving forward, they begin to build resilience instead of fear. Rising above failure is rarely about avoiding mistakes. It is about learning how to stand back up, re center, and keep choosing growth, one deliberate step at a time.

Once young people learn that failure does not define them, a deeper question emerges: Who am I becoming, and how do I use my voice as I move forward?

Reflection Question:

What might change, at home, at school, or within yourself, if failure were treated not as an ending, but as part of the path forward?

Chapter Ten

Influence Youth to Discover Purpose and Use Their Voice Wisely

"Your voice is not just a sound—it is a responsibility."
~ Dr. Danita Johnson Woods

When Voice Meets Purpose

Every young person has a voice. But not every voice is grounded in purpose.

In a world that rewards immediacy, volume, and reaction, young people are often encouraged to speak before they have had the time or support to understand what they stand for. Expression is celebrated, but discernment is rarely taught. As a result, voice can become performance rather than leadership, and influence can drift without direction.

This chapter explores how purpose gives voice weight—and how learning when to speak, when to listen, and when to pause can shape not only what young people say, but who they become. Influence, at its best, is not about being heard the most. It is about being aligned with something that matters.

The Mic Was On

She didn't realize the microphone was live.

Standing just offstage at a youth leadership forum, she was rehearsing—half whisper, half prayer. Not a speech. Not something polished.

Just a reminder to herself: *Don't mess this up. Say something that matters.*

When she stepped forward, the room went quiet—the kind of quiet that feels heavier than noise. She paused, smiled nervously, and said, "I was practicing what I wanted to say… and I guess you heard it."

Laughter softened the moment. Then her tone shifted.

"I used to think having a voice meant being loud. Or being right. Or being noticed. But what I've learned is this: your voice means very little if you don't know what you're standing on."

She spoke about failure. About trying to sound confident while feeling unsure. About learning that influence without purpose feels empty, like speaking into a room you don't yet belong in.

When she finished, the applause came—but quieter than expected. More thoughtful.

Later, a younger student approached her and said, "I didn't know you were allowed to think before you speak."

That unrehearsed moment became the most powerful thing she said all day.

Not because the mic was on.

But because her purpose was.

The Weight a Voice Carries

Words have consequences.

They always have.

A voice can:

- Encourage or discourage
- Heal or harden
- Clarify or confuse
- Protect or expose

Young people need help understanding that speaking carries weight, even when it feels casual, even when it happens online, even when it is framed as "just an opinion."

Silence carries weight, too.

There are moments when silence protects dignity, preserves safety, or creates space for learning. There are also moments when silence enables harm. Wisdom lies in knowing the difference.

That discernment does not come naturally. It must be modeled, taught, and practiced. Especially in a culture that rewards immediacy, young people need to learn that pause is not weakness, it is maturity.

Learning When to Speak—and When to Listen

Not every thought needs a microphone.

Not every reaction deserves an audience.

Listening is leadership.

Reflection is courage.

Young people need permission to slow down and ask:

- Why do I want to say this?
- Who does this help?
- What happens after I speak?

Helping youth develop emotional regulation before expression is one of the most important protective skills we can offer. A voice guided by impulse may feel powerful in the moment, but a voice guided by intention has lasting impact.

This is especially critical in a digital world where reaction is rewarded and restraint is often misunderstood. As explored earlier, platforms may amplify voices, but purpose determines how they are used.

Purpose Is Discovered Through Action, Not Declaration

Many young people believe they must find their purpose before they can act.

The truth is the opposite.

Purpose is revealed through action:

- Volunteering
- Mentoring
- Leading small efforts
- Serving quietly
- Trying—and sometimes failing

Each experience refines understanding. Each step clarifies direction.

Adults can support this process by creating opportunities rather than pressuring outcomes. Encourage engagement. Encourage contribution. Encourage reflection. Purpose grows where responsibility is practiced.

A Story of Discernment

I once worked with a young man who was passionate, articulate, and deeply frustrated by injustice. He spoke often, and forcefully. His words drew attention, but over time they created distance. People heard him, but they stopped listening.

A mentor asked him a simple question:

"What do you want your words to build?"

That question changed everything.

He began listening more than speaking. He asked questions before making statements. He learned when silence created space—and when speaking could create change.

His voice didn't disappear.
It matured.

Purpose didn't quiet him.

It refined him.

Using Your Voice with Intention

- *Purpose gives voice direction*
- *Listening is leadership*
- *Pause before reacting*
- *Ask who benefits from your words*
- *Remember: impact lasts longer than applause*

Teaching Voice as Responsibility

A voice is not neutral. It carries weight whether the speaker intends it to or not.

Leadership begins when young people understand that their words can shape rooms, redirect conversations, and influence outcomes long after the moment has passed. Teaching voice as responsibility is not about limiting expression; it is about expanding awareness.

Too often, young people are taught how to speak—presentation skills, debate techniques, persuasive language—without being taught when to speak, why to speak, or what silence can protect. Without that context, voice becomes performance rather than practice.

Responsible voice requires discernment. It asks young people to consider whether they are speaking to be heard or speaking to be helpful. It reframes influence not as power over others, but as stewardship on behalf of something larger than self.

Leaders do not speak simply because they can.

They speak because the moment requires integrity.

Teaching voice as responsibility also invites accountability. When young people understand that their words matter, they begin to own their impact—not just their intent. They learn to revise, when necessary, apologize when needed, and listen as carefully as they speak. These are not weaknesses. They are leadership muscles.

When purpose anchors voice and responsibility guides expression, young people begin to lead long before they hold a title.

Guiding Youth Toward Responsible Expression

Adults shape how young people use their voices by what we model—and what we tolerate.

We can:

- Affirm thoughtful expression
- Challenge harmful rhetoric without shaming
- Teach disagreement without disrespect
- Encourage courage paired with care

Influence grows through dialogue, not control.

Soul Pause

When Voice Meets Purpose

Pause for a moment and think about a time your voice mattered more than you realized.

What did you say?

What did you mean to communicate?
What impact did your words have, intended or not?

Now think about a young person you influence.

Are they learning that speaking is the same as leading?
Are they being rewarded for volume more than wisdom?
Do they know they are allowed to pause before they perform?

Breathe here.

Purpose does not demand a microphone.
It demands alignment.

A wise voice asks first:
Why am I speaking?
Who will this help?
What will this build after the moment passes?

Let this be a quiet commitment:
Model the pause.
Model the listening.
Model the courage to speak only when your words can carry care.

Closing Callback: *What the Room Heard*

At the end of the day, the microphone does not decide what matters. The moment does.

Long after the applause fades and platforms change, what remains is not how loudly a young person spoke, but whether their words were anchored in purpose and carried with care.

Every room is listening—whether the mic is on or not.

What young people are learning through our guidance, our example, and our restraint is how to stand on something solid before they speak. When they do, their voice no longer searches for permission. It arrives with clarity.

Because when purpose leads and responsibility follows, even quiet words can change a room.

Closing Reflection

Young people do not need fewer voices—they need wiser ones.

They need guidance in understanding that their words matter because they matter.

That purpose is not proven by volume, but by alignment.

And that influence, at its best, is rooted in care for others as much as conviction within oneself.

Skill without purpose is noise.

Skill guided by meaning becomes influence.

Reflection Question

How might our communities change if we taught young people not just how to speak—but how to listen, reflect, and use their voices with purpose?

Chapter Eleven

Influence Youth to Use AI as a Tool for Growth, Not a Crutch

"The future doesn't belong to the loudest voices or the fastest clicks. It belongs to those who learn how to think, adapt, and apply wisdom to powerful tools."
~ Dr. Danita Johnson Woods

Purpose gives direction, but direction still needs tools.

In earlier chapters, we explored how young people learn what to value, how digital forces quietly shape their thinking, and why discovering purpose and using one's voice wisely matters more than ever. Yet purpose alone is not enough. In a world increasingly shaped by technology, young people must also learn how to navigate power, who controls it, how it is distributed, and how they can access it without losing themselves in the process.

Artificial intelligence is one of those forces of power.

Once confined to research labs and elite institutions, AI now sits in the palms of our children's hands. It writes, calculates, designs, tutors, analyzes, organizes, and predicts. Used well, it can close gaps in learning, unlock opportunity, and accelerate growth. Used poorly, or blindly, it can reinforce dependency, distort thinking, and quietly replace effort with imitation.

This chapter is not about chasing the newest apps or glorifying technology as a solution to every problem. It is about agency. About teaching young people, especially those who have historically been left out of systems of advantage, how to use intelligent tools intentionally, ethically, and in service of who they are becoming.

For many young people, particularly young men, the challenge is not a lack of ability. It is a lack of guidance. They are surrounded by digital tools but rarely taught how to use them to build skill, confidence, or credibility. Instead, technology often becomes entertainment, escape, or distraction, another algorithm deciding rather than empowering.

But tools are not destiny.

As we saw in Chapter Seven, digital influence shapes what young people see and believe. As we explored in Chapter Ten, purpose gives meaning to effort and direction to voice. This chapter sits at the intersection of those truths. It asks a practical question with profound implications:

How can today's youth use intelligent tools to strengthen, not substitute, their thinking, discipline, and sense of purpose?

Because skill without purpose is noise.

And skill guided by meaning becomes influence.

What follows is not a promise of shortcuts, but an invitation to mastery, one tool, one decision, one intention at a time.

AI as a Personal Learning Partner

One of the greatest advantages AI offers young people is access to individualized learning. Many students, especially boys, struggle in environments that reward speed, compliance, or one size fits all instruction. AI driven tools can help break that pattern by allowing learners to move at their own pace, revisit concepts without embarrassment, and receive immediate feedback.

AI can help explain complex material in simpler language, generate practice problems, and offer alternative ways to understand difficult concepts. It does not judge. It does not compare. It simply responds.

For youth who have quietly decided they are "not good at school," this alone can be transformative.

But here is the critical distinction: AI can support learning. It cannot replace the responsibility to learn. The goal is not to outsource thinking, but to strengthen it.

AI as a Career Scout and Skill Builder

Many young men struggle not because they lack ability, but because they lack direction. AI can help bridge that gap by exposing youth to career pathways they may never see in their immediate environment, careers that align with how they think, what they enjoy, and how they learn.

AI tools can help young people:

- Explore career options based on interests and strengths
- Understand which skills lead to real employment opportunities
- Identify alternatives to traditional four-year college pathways
- Begin developing marketable skills early

From coding and digital design to data analysis, video editing, and entrepreneurship, AI can act as a guide, helping youth practice, trouble shoot, and refine skills that translate into real world value.

This is especially important for young men who are hands on learners or who thrive when they can see tangible outcomes. Skills build confidence. Confidence builds momentum.

Marcus Finds a Different Way In

Marcus was seventeen and already convinced that school "wasn't for him."

He wasn't failing outright, but he was drifting, turning in work late, skipping assignments, sitting quietly in the back of class counting the minutes until the bell rang. Teachers described him as capable but unmotivated. Marcus described himself as bored.

What no one had asked him, until a mentor did, was how he liked to learn.

Marcus spent hours online watching videos about cars, sneakers, and business owners who built brands from scratch. When his mentor introduced him to AI tools that could help him analyze business ideas, draft plans, and learn basic coding and design, something shifted. For the first time, learning felt connected to his curiosity, not imposed on it.

He began using AI to break down assignments, practice writing in his own voice, and explore careers in logistics and digital marketing. It didn't make the work effortless, but it made it possible. More importantly, it helped Marcus see himself not as "behind," but as becoming.

The tool didn't change Marcus.

Awareness, guidance, and purpose did.

Guiding Youth to Use AI Wisely

For Parents, Mentors, and Educators

- *Don't ask only what they are using. Ask why. Curiosity reveals more than control.*
- *Frame AI as a tool, not a shortcut. Reinforce effort, thinking, and accountability.*
- *Set expectations around integrity. Explain the difference between assistance and substitution.*
- *Encourage creation, not just consumption. Writing, designing, building, and problem solving matter.*

- *Model discernment. How adults talk about technology teaches youth how to value it.*
- *Connect tools to purpose. Skills grow fastest when young people see meaning in what they are learning.*

AI doesn't raise children.
Adults still do.

AI as a Communication and Confidence Coach

Communication is one of the most underestimated barriers facing young people today. Many struggle to express ideas clearly, write professionally, or advocate for themselves effectively. AI tools can help youth practice writing, prepare for interviews, draft resumes, and refine their tone, skills that often determine access to opportunity.

When used responsibly, AI can help young people find their voice, not replace it. It can assist in organizing thoughts, improving clarity, and translating ideas into action. Over time, this builds confidence, not dependency, if guided correctly.

The Discipline Question

Here is where influence matters most.

AI can help young people plan goals, manage time, and break large tasks into manageable steps. But it cannot supply discipline where none exists. In fact, AI often amplifies existing habits. For a focused learner, it accelerates progress. For a distracted one, it becomes another excuse to avoid effort.

Young people must be taught this truth clearly:

AI rewards intention.

It exposes avoidance.

Without structure, values, and accountability, even the most advanced tools will lead nowhere.

A Necessary Caution

AI is not neutral in its impact. Used improperly, it can:

- Encourage shortcuts over mastery
- Replace effort with convenience
- Reinforce isolation rather than growth
- Undermine critical thinking

This is why adults, parents, mentors, and educators, cannot abdicate their role. Young people do not need unrestricted access. They need guided exposure. They need conversations about ethics, integrity, and responsibility. They need role models who demonstrate that tools serve values, not the other way around.

Purpose Is the Difference

Technology alone does not create direction. Purpose does.

When young people understand why they are learning, who they want to become, and how their efforts connect to something larger than themselves, AI becomes a ladder rather than a trap.

Without purpose, AI is noise.

With purpose, it becomes leverage.

Tools, Thought, and Intention

Pause for a moment and think about a tool that once made something easier for you.

Did it strengthen your ability, or quietly replace effort?
Did it help you grow, or tempt you to skip a step that mattered?

Now consider the young people in your life.

Are they learning how to think with tools, or how to lean on them?
Do they know the difference between support and substitution?
Have they been shown that effort still matters, even when assistance is instant?

Breathe here.

Powerful tools do not remove responsibility.
They reveal it.

Growth does not come from access alone.
It comes from intention, discipline, and purpose guiding what is available.

Every pause you model before using a tool becomes permission for a young person to lead their future rather than outsource it.

Closing Reflection

The future will not belong to those with the most advanced technology. It will belong to those who learn how to use technology wisely, ethically, and with restraint.

AI will not replace young people, but young people who learn to work with AI thoughtfully will expand their possibilities in ways previous generations could not imagine.

The responsibility now rests with us: to influence youth not merely to keep up, but to grow strong, skilled, and grounded in a rapidly changing world.

Reflection Question:

How might a young person's life change if they learned early that tools do not define their future, but how they choose to use them does?

Chapter Twelve

Influence the Future Today

"You don't have to be a 'person of influence' to be influential. In fact, the most influential people in my life are probably not even aware of the things they've taught me."
~Scott Adams

Today's youth are our future, and they need caring adults who are willing to influence them toward positive paths. Contrary to popular belief, this responsibility does not rest solely with parents or educators. Shaping the next generation is a shared responsibility, one that belongs to all of us.

We've heard the saying, "It takes a village to raise a child."

You are part of that village.

Whenever I encourage parents, educators, and community members to step into the role of positive influence, I often hear responses like:

"Why me?"

"I can't."

"That's not my role."

I respectfully disagree. In fact, let's address and reframe the most common reasons people give for holding back.

"I'm not the right person to influence a child."

You may feel you don't know enough to offer wisdom or guidance. You may believe you need to achieve a certain level of success, or have everything figured out, before you can help someone else.

That assumption simply isn't true.

You don't need a perfect life or all the answers. You only need to be one step ahead of someone else. Your experiences, both successes and struggles, carry insight that can be valuable to a young person navigating life for the first time.

"No child would ever listen to me."

You might be right. Not every child will listen immediately. But influence is not limited to formal mentoring relationships. Sometimes influence looks like:

- Modeling integrity
- Demonstrating kindness
- Showing up consistently
- Offering a moment of encouragement

You don't need to fill every role in a child's life. Start where you are. Do what you can. Over time, trust can grow, and so can your impact.

"I don't have time."

Life is busy. Responsibilities compete for our attention. But influence does not require a formal commitment or scheduled meetings.

Some of the most meaningful moments happen casually:

- A short text message of encouragement
- A thoughtful email
- A warm greeting or brief conversation

Small gestures can send a powerful message: You matter.

"I don't know any kids."

Young people are everywhere, and many are eager for guidance, encouragement, and support. You can engage through your existing network or connect with organizations seeking volunteers, mentors, and advocates.

Organizations such as My Brother's Keeper, My Sister's Keeper, Boys and Girls Clubs of America, and VolunteerMatch provide opportunities to have an influence in ways that align with your interests and availability.

"I'll give more than I receive."

Influence should never feel burdensome or one sided. Healthy influence includes clear boundaries and mutual respect. When those are in place, the rewards are significant.

You gain purpose.

You gain perspective.

You gain confidence as you witness the positive impact of your presence.

With a new perspective, influencing youth becomes a shared journey, one that benefits both the adult and the child.

The Quiet Power of Influence

Influence does not always announce itself.
Often, it works beneath the surface, unnoticed, unnamed, and unmeasured.

A calm response in a tense moment.
A boundary held with compassion.
A standard modeled without explanation.

Children absorb these details long before they understand their significance.
What feels ordinary to you may become foundational to them.

Influence grows not from grand gestures, but from repeated, intentional presence.

Being a positive influence isn't about control or direction alone. It's about nurturing a child's natural strengths, helping them grow into confident, capable, and contributing adults.

Growth takes time. Start small. Build gradually. Small wins create momentum and confidence.

Children learn best by doing and observing. Model the behaviors you hope to see. Invite participation. Encourage effort over perfection.

And resist the urge to do everything for them.

Allowing children to make mistakes, while offering guidance and support, builds resilience. The goal is balance, not abandonment and not over rescue. Each child is different. Pay attention. Adjust as needed.

An Intentional Approach to Influence

It's easy to underestimate the effect we have on children. We often assume they are resilient enough to "bounce back" from what they see. While resilience is real, children are also deeply observant. They absorb far more than we realize.

That's why influence should be intentional.

Intentional influence means living with awareness, understanding that our choices, behaviors, and attitudes shape more than just our own lives.

Intentional influence includes:

- Being proactive
  Take responsibility for your actions and model accountability.
- Having a dream
  Protect your own vision and help keep children's dreams alive.
- Aligning values and priorities
  Know what you stand for, and live it consistently.

- Looking beyond yourself
  Seek outcomes that benefit everyone involved.
- Filling emotional accounts
  Invest in relationships with patience, trust, and encouragement, while also caring for yourself.

Ultimately, intentional influence is about staying awake to the impact we have on the world, and on the children watching us.

Yes, You Have What It Takes to Be a Positive Influence

Throughout my personal and professional life, I've witnessed the power of influence from both sides. From these experiences, I've observed key traits shared by those who make the greatest difference.

Great influencers are:

1. Credible. Honest, reliable, and willing to learn alongside others
2. Positive. Aware of how their attitude affects those around them
3. Genuinely Interested. Motivated by care, not obligation
4. Open Sharers. Using stories to teach and connect
5. Thoughtful Questioners. Seeking meaning, not surface answers
6. Perspective Givers. Offering clarity without judgment
7. Empathetic Listeners. Listening first, solving second

Influence isn't about having all the answers. It's about helping others discover their own.

Make Your Move

In my role as CEO of Edgewater Health, I've seen how the right influence, at the right time, can change lives. I've witnessed individuals overcome addiction, professionals mentor the next generation, and even children influence one another toward better choices.

No one succeeds alone.

We are relational by design. We grow stronger through connection. Yet today's culture often celebrates self sufficiency at the expense of community.

Personal responsibility matters, but so does support.

We must normalize asking for help. We must remove the stigma attached to needing guidance. And we must recommit to showing up for one another, especially for our youth.

If this chapter stirred something in you, listen to it.

Be present.

Be intentional.

Be a positive influence, starting today.

Our future depends on it.

The Influence You Don't See

Pause for a moment and think about someone who influenced you quietly.

They may not have lectured you.
They may not have mentored you formally.
They may not even know the role they played.

What did they model?
How did they make you feel—seen, capable, or safe?

Now consider your own life.

Who is watching how you respond under pressure?
Who is learning from how you treat others when no one is keeping score?
What message does your consistency send?

Breathe here.

Influence is not loud.
It is lived.

Every small choice you make becomes instruction for someone else.
Every act of presence becomes permission for growth.

Closing Reflection

Influence is not about position, perfection, or proximity.

It is about presence.

It is about who you are when no one is watching, and who you choose to be when someone is.

Children are always watching.

Not for flawless behavior, but for authentic humanity.

Every generation is shaped, in part, by ordinary adults who decided to show up anyway.

Who chose consistency over convenience.

Who understood that small moments, repeated with intention, build lasting impact.

You don't have to change the world.

You only have to influence the piece of it within your reach.

And that is more than enough.

Final Question

Who might be watching you more closely than you realize, and what example are you setting, intentionally or unintentionally, through your everyday choices?

Acknowledgments

This book exists because of the many people who have shaped my life, challenged my thinking, and walked alongside me through seasons of growth, failure, and renewal.

First, I thank my parents and my grandmother, Daisy. Your lives, lessons, and quiet strength planted the earliest seeds of the ideas explored in these pages. Your influence continues to guide my work and my values.

To my husband, Michael—thank you for your unwavering encouragement, perspective, and partnership. Your belief in me and your steadiness remain a foundation I carry with me. To my daughter, Kyla, and my grandchildren, thank you for your patience, love, and constant support. You are a daily reminder of what truly matters.

I am especially grateful to my first-grade teacher, Mrs. Gussie Kaufman. Your early belief in me mattered more than you may ever know, and I carry those lessons forward in how I see and support others.

I also extend sincere thanks to those who shared their time, insight, and stories in service of this book, including my grandson, Javier Cardona, Dr. Steve Simpson, Dr. Rachel Ross, Special Agent Mike Prendergast, and Brandon Freeland. Your experiences and perspectives strengthened this work and reinforced the importance of thoughtful, intentional influence.

To the Edgewater Health team. Your daily commitment to children, families, and communities continues to inspire me. You demonstrate, through action, what is possible when people are seen, supported, and given the opportunity to thrive—even in the most challenging circumstances.

About the Author

Dr. Danita Johnson Woods is a healthcare executive, author, speaker, and community leader whose work centers on leadership, accountability, and the power of intentional influence.

Her professional journey is rooted in lived experience and sustained by education, discipline, and purpose. Early challenges did not define her trajectory, they sharpened it. Through perseverance and personal responsibility, Dr. Woods transformed adversity into a foundation for leadership and service.

She holds a Bachelor's and Master's degree in Public Administration from Indiana University Northwest, a Master's degree in Social Service Administration and a Graduate Certificate in Health Administration & Policy from the University of Chicago, and a Ph.D. in Human Services from Walden University.

Dr. Woods currently serves as President and CEO of Edgewater Health, an integrated healthcare system serving Northwest Indiana. She is widely recognized for leading organizational transformation, expanding access to care, and building systems that prioritize dignity, accountability, and outcomes.

Through her writing, speaking, and executive leadership, Dr. Woods challenges individuals and institutions to pay attention to the details that shape lives, communities, and futures. Her work emphasizes that influence is not about position or volume—but about consistency, character, and care.

She lives in Indiana and is the proud matriarch of a blended family that includes one daughter, two sons, and several grandchildren. She was married to Michael Woods, whose love, partnership, and encouragement remain a lasting part of her life and work.

Speaking & Engagements

Dr. Danita Johnson Woods is available for keynote presentations, leadership talks, and facilitated conversations designed to inspire clarity, responsibility, and meaningful action.

She delivers customized **30–60 minute keynote presentations** on topics including:

- Leadership and accountability
- Purpose, voice, and influence
- Resilience and personal responsibility
- Mentorship and community impact

Dr. Woods has spoken to diverse audiences, including educators, healthcare professionals, leadership organizations, civic groups, non-profit leaders, faith-based communities, and emerging changemakers.

Speaking engagements are typically **paid professional keynotes**. A limited number of no-fee engagements are reserved annually for mission-aligned nonprofit or community organizations.

To inquire about a speaking engagement, please include:

- Type of event (keynote, panel, workshop)
- Event title and theme
- Date, location, and format (in-person or virtual)
- Audience size and demographics
- Other speakers or organizations involved

Contact:

info@drdanitajohnsonwoods.com

For additional information, books, and resources, please visit:

www.drdanitajohnsonwoods.com

www.ingramcontent.com/pod-product-compliance
Lightning Source LLC
LaVergne TN
LVHW021140160826
845679LV00023B/1981

* 9 7 9 8 9 9 4 8 2 8 0 0 7 *